INDIVIDUAL
AND COMMUNITY

INDIVIDUAL AND COMMUNITY

The Rise of the *Polis*
800–500 B.C.

Chester G. Starr

New York   Oxford
OXFORD UNIVERSITY PRESS
1986

Oxford University Press

Oxford   New York   Toronto
Delhi   Bombay   Calcutta   Madras   Karachi
Petaling Jaya   Singapore   Hong Kong   Tokyo
Nairobi   Dar es Salaam   Cape Town
Melbourne   Auckland

and associated companies in
Beirut   Berlin   Ibadan   Nicosia

Copyright © 1986 by Oxford University Press, Inc.

Published by Oxford University Press, Inc.,
200 Madison Avenue, New York, New York 10016

Oxford is a registered trademark of Oxford University Press

Library of Congress Cataloging-in-Publication Data

Starr, Chester G., 1914-
Individual and community.

Bibliography: p.
Includes index.
1. Greece—Politics and government—To 146 B.C.
I. Title.
JC73.S68   1986   320.938   85-15360
ISBN 0-19-503971-8

Printing (last digit):   9 8 7 6 5 4 3 2 1

Printed in the United States of America

To my beloved wife
Gretchen

Preface

During the three centuries from 800 to 500 B.C., the Greek world moved from a primitive cultural and economic level to one in which its artistic products dominated all Mediterranean markets, supported by a wide overseas trade to a far-flung web of colonies; in the two following centuries came the literary, philosophical, and artistic masterpieces of the classical era. Vital in this advance was a parallel political progress, the crystallization and consolidation of the *polis* as a system of government in which citizens had rights as well as duties under the rule of law, a system hitherto unknown in human history. As the great historian W. S. Ferguson succinctly put it, "The *polis* was a hothouse for Greek civilization."

Throughout the period to be treated in the following pages there was an enduring tension between the demands of the individual for his own glory and honor and the less vocally expressed needs of the community. At the beginning stands the Homeric world with self-willed heroes; at its end, the perfected *polis* of 500 B.C. This conflict gives structure to any analysis of the stages of development; despite open friction and at times a lack of balance, the Greeks hammered out a brilliant compromise to a problem which many societies have faced less successfully. By 500 the community had attained a political unity through which common ends could be achieved, and yet the human beings who populated the *poleis* could feel themselves significant in their own right. This must be a major theme in the following discussion, as suggested by my title; but no phase of history can be comprehended simply in terms of such antitheses. The rise of the *polis* requires consideration of many other factors as well, social, religious, and economic in nature.

In various books and articles I have examined parts of this remarkable story, but it is time to treat them together in an integrated study. Inasmuch as one of my earlier books discusses in detail the economic and social growth of Greece during the same period, let me make it clear that the present treatment is in no way intended as a companion but rather stands on its own.

The evidence for the wide range of issues which will face us is not as voluminous as one would wish. Apart from the Homeric epics and two long poems of Hesiod, the only corpus of poetry which survives entire is that passing under the name of Theognis; the first prose work is the history of Herodotus, who looked back occasionally—and very usefully—into the sixth century. This material, together with the physical remains which are sometimes of critical importance, does illuminate the main stages of progress, but is not always adequately varied to permit a full depiction of all the compexities which attend any great historical upheaval.

Many other students have meditated on one aspect or another of Greek political evolution; in my notes I cite the most relevant accounts, but it would be impossible to give a full bibliography on any topic. All historical work rests upon the labors of many predecessors, not always of the most recent generation and not always visible on the surface.

Ann Arbor, Michigan   C. G. S.
October, 1985

Contents

I   Land, Sea, and Sun   **3**

Geography and Climate, 4   A Rural World, 6   The Shining
Sea, 9   Rise and Fall of the Early Aegean World, 10

II   An Age of Chieftains   **15**

Tribes and Chieftains, 16   Political Procedures in the *Iliad*,
18   The Power of the *Basileus*, 21   The Beginnings of
Change: The *Odyssey* and Hesiod, 24   Social Structure and
Values, 27

III   Crystallization of the *Polis*   **34**

Appearance of the *Polis*, 35   The Physical Evidence, 37
Anthropological Models, 42   The Early *Polis*, 46

IV   Patriotism and Divisiveness   **52**

The Demands of War, 53   Consolidation of Government,
55   The Aristocratic Way of Life, 59   Aristocratic Search
for Wealth, 63

V   Upheaval and Reform   **67**

Cities, Coins and Thinkers, 69   Reforms: Sparta and
Athens, 74   Tyrants, 80

VI   The *Polis* World in 500 B.C.   **87**

Athenian Democracy, 89   Greek Oligarchies, 93   The
Perfected *Polis,* 97

Notes   **101**
Bibliography   **127**
Index   **131**

INDIVIDUAL
AND COMMUNITY

CHAPTER I

Land, Sea, and Sun

Once Athens was famous for its pellucid air and blinding sunshine; standing on the Acropolis in the years before the Second World War one could look out over a rocky, brush-covered landscape to the shimmering sea at the Piraeus. Now any visitor to Athens endures the car-choked streets of a major metropolis, and must inhale its heavily polluted air when he inspects the deteriorating monuments of the Acropolis; to the south his gaze is hemmed by range after range of apartment buildings beyond which the sea can rarely be seen. It is almost impossible to visualize the hamlet with minarets 150 years ago when the Greeks were shaking off Turkish rule; or the small ancient city of Athens, which itself was not highly praised. "The city of Athens," noted a traveler of the third century B.C., "is very drought-ridden; its water supplies are inadequate, and being so ancient a town it is badly planned. A stranger, coming on it unawares, might well doubt whether this could be the city of the Athenians."[1]

Leaving behind the bedlam of modern Athens, one finds the countryside equally changed. A plant manufacturing plastic items has replaced the cotton and tomato crops of a Boeotian plain; women no longer work the fields clad in shapeless black dresses, formerly required by mourning for relatives dead far too young; the mountain villages are being abandoned.[2] In city and country alike there has been more visible change in the past generation than for centuries.

Accordingly the effort of various recent studies to draw parallels between ancient and modern Hellenic values and ways of life, even in rural contexts, is hazardous, often misleading.[3] Since antiquity there have been centuries of Byzantine and then Turkish rule; the Greek orthodox faith has provided a sure base for its adherents. One need only read a menu in a taverna, with its pilaf and other dishes of Near Eastern origin, to sense the deep changes; so too demotic Greek exhibits a broken-down grammar and widely adulterated vocabulary (though ancient Greek, for that matter, had a considerable stock of words not of Indo-European origin). Greeks today often have an insatiable curiosity harnessed to a lively mind—even in remote villages—but that cannot be taken as a genetic inheritance from their distant ancestors. The next chapter will consider the dependent position of women in ancient times, the unity of the family—the honor (*time*) of which had to be upheld at all costs—and a variety of social factors which much resemble those still dominating Aegean life, urban though it now is; a modern New Year's wish is "male children, female lambs."[4] Similarities in customs and values may reflect fundamental constants in village life, but they do not prove historical continuity.

Geography and Climate

There are physical factors which have always had a wide range of effects on the population of the Aegean.[5] Yet even here one must be cautious in generalizing. The great tectonic movements of geological plates which shoved up the heights of eastern Attica took place long ago, but in the historical period various changes have altered the landscape. As in other parts of the Mediterranean basin, river valleys have silted up and have extended the coastline; once upon a time the sea lapped the edge of Ephesus, which now lies several miles inland. Elevation and still more subsidence of the coast are evident at Corinth, Porto Cheli, and elsewhere. The hillsides, too, were more heavily forested in antiquity; depredations of voracious goats and charcoal-burners have stripped them of all their cover save prickly bushes which support only bees. By the fourth century B.C. Plato described Attica virtually as it is today, a decayed carcass with the bare bones sticking out through the skin, though one of his contemporaries

every day sent assloads of wood to stoke the Athenian braziers
(*Critias* 111c).[6]

Throughout the long millennia of human habitation, mainland Greece has been a region mainly of limestone mountains
which have sunk at their southern end. Where they meet the
main bulk of the Balkans the mountains still stand tall and are
bordered by the major plains of Macedonia and Thessaly. In the
south the sea sends long fingers up between the mountain ridges;
and the plains, which are small, are sometimes landlocked valleys, sometimes narrow coastal strips. The Saronic gulf and the
gulf of Corinth in particular almost separate the Peloponnesus
from central Greece. Along the eastern fringes of the Aegean the
coastal districts of Asia Minor are more extensive, and are tra-
versed by rivers such as the Hermus and Maeander, which break
down from the plateau of Anatolia through rocky ridges.

For the purposes of ancient industry Greece was reasonably
well equipped with natural resources. Stone is to be found everywhere; the Pentelic marble of Attica and some of the island mar-
bles were highly prized, but any stone could be worked into ar-
chitectural members and then plastered and painted. Good clay
beds are abundant, especially at Corinth and Athens, though Aegina always had to depend on imported clay. Veins of silver, copper, and other metals are also present; only timber, tin, and to
some degree wool needed to be found elsewhere.

The Mediterranean climate does not seem to have altered ap-
preciably in recent geologic times.[7] Since rain falls mainly in the
winter, the agricultural calendar revolves around the cultivation
of winter crops; only where there is irrigation, not much practiced in a land with seasonal rainfall, can summer vegetables be
raised.[8] In the summer, as the poet Hesiod put it, "the chirping
grasshopper sits in a tree and pours down his shrill song con-
tinually from under his wings in the season of wearisome heat,
then goats are plumpest and wine sweetest; women are most
wanton, but men are feeblest, because Sirius parches head and
knees and the skin is dry through heat" (*Works and Days* 582–
88). Even in the winter, however, the climate is moderated by the
encircling seas, as compared to the harshness of northern Europe,

so that human needs for heat are reduced and outdoor life remains possible, at least in coastal districts.

Within the common climatic pattern there is an extraordinary range of variations for so small a land. The western shore of the mainland has up to three times as much rain as the plains of Attica, where dust storms scourge the landscape day after day in the summer. At Arcadian Bassae snow lingers until late March, and statuettes depict mountain shepherds huddled in heavy cloaks. At least once the sacred procession of the City Dionysia at Athens in early spring had to be cancelled because of an unusually late and severe frost; and Hesiod bitterly describes his home village of Ascra on the slopes of Mount Helicon as "bad in winter, sultry in summer, and good at no time" (*Works and Days* 640). One may doubt that the clarity of the atmosphere really promoted the unfolding of the Hellenic miracle or that, as Aristotle put it, the Aegean population "intermediate in geographical position . . . possesses both spirit and intelligence," yet a modern Westerner often feels exhilarated on entering into Greece.[9]

A Rural World

As late as 1950 almost half of the Greek people lived in a multiplicity of rural communes (5473 to be exact), and in antiquity certainly 80% to 90% of the population was rurally based. In the United States 94.9% resided on farms in 1790; and the reasons for agricultural predominance in antiquity were even more compelling, for only specially fertile areas could produce a significant surplus for non-farming elements. Not until seaborne grain became available in the sixth and following centuries did true cities emerge.

A resident of the United States consumes about 2700 calories per day; ancient Greeks, who were usually of Mediterranean body type and younger on the average, probably needed no more than 2000 calories.[10] These would have been gained largely from cereals—primarily barley and, only secondarily, wheat. The former grew better in the Greek climate, and in later centuries cost about half as much as wheat. It was used mainly in broth; in the time of Solon wheaten bread was provided at the public Prytane-ion only on feast days.[11] Grain requirements for an average man have been calculated at six *medimnoi* (three hectoliters) of wheat per year. Even today a peasant can say, "Bread is our only food. It is our milk, cheese, butter, honey, sugar, all in one. What the grass is to the animal, bread is to us. Otherwise we live on air and water."[12]

Actually, however, the ancient diet included fruits such as figs and grapes, wine, olive oil, and some vegetables, especially le-gumes, which provided protein (also available in cheese) and fixed nitrogen in the soil. Fish was not as common an item as often asserted; Aegean waters are too clear, too devoid of plant life, to support large schools of edible fish. Meat was consumed mainly at the barbecues held during public sacrifices. One must not forget, also, that all early societies gathered and ate a variety of wild plants which were not raised as crops.[13]

Ancient agricultural yields can only be set in a general range. In modern times the average for Greece has been about 13 hecto-liters of wheat per hectare and 20 to 24 for barley; in antiquity it was probably smaller. A cultivated hectare would provide grain for perhaps less than three persons, allowing for seed reserves, wastage, and animal feed. If an average family size is arbitrarily estimated at four and it is assumed that half the cropland re-mained fallow each year, then a farmer with two hectares could scarcely have supported his family. Dependent almost entirely on hand labor, he could not have cultivated more than four hect-ares unless he drew in outside labor at critical points in the agri-cultural cycle—activities such as harvesting (six days per hectare) had to take place at a specific time and could not be delayed. The upper levels of the agricultural population enjoyed the fruits of some 15 to 30 hectares; a sizeable part of the villagers (*thetes*), on the other hand, either held no land or only a small plot and pro-vided a reservoir of labor for the seasonal demands of their richer neighbors.[14]

Rural inhabitants, at least down into the fourth century B.C., lived almost entirely in villages. Water supply "in the season of wearisome heat" required everflowing springs, for the minor creeks dried up; in early days, too, physical security depended on local group protection. The size of these villages was limited by a constant still operative in Greek agricultural life: farmers preferred not to have to trudge more than half an hour, or at most an hour, to their fields.[15]

Human life in ancient times was also marked by ineluctable demographic factors which have been present everywhere in history until recent times. Infant mortality probably ran over 200 per 1000; death rates in adulthood were also higher than in the modern world, both because illnesses could easily become fatal and also because males, engaged in harsh physical labor, died, worn out, before their time. Life expectancy at birth must have been in the range of 30 to 35 years; women, subject to the dangers of childbirth, died somewhat earlier than men as a rule. Even so, better nourished male citizens who reached the age of 35 could expect another 20 to 25 years of life; obligations of military service usually ran to 60, and Solon spoke of a man's career as stretching to the age of 70.[16]

The consequences of these conditions radiated far. Over one-third the inhabitants of any state were under 15; the tenacious elders were few and perhaps therefore, like the garrulous but wise Nestor, more respected. Few Greeks in their right mind, however, would have agreed with Rabbi Ben Ezra's exhortation, "Grow old along with me! The best is yet to be." Plato quotes no less than five times an Attic drinking song, "It is best . . . to be young with friends," and the early poets proclaimed old age to be worse than death.[17] In such a society, group preservation was more important than individual self-assertion—and so the presence of this phenomenon at any point or in any class is the more worthy of note—but a family could not count with any certainty on the production of males who would carry on its rites and inherit its *kleros* or farm, possession of which, as will appear later, was intimately linked to the rights of citizenship. The combination of demographic forces essentially produced an equilibrium in which a rapid explosion of population could scarcely be expected; Hesiod even advises his auditors to have no more than one son to ensure the undivided transmission of the family estate.[18]

The Shining Sea

Thus far we have looked principally at mainland Greece, which was to be the major center for the historical evolution of the *polis* and of Greek culture generally. Concentration on this focus has its dangers; "Greece" is best comprehended as a sea, the Aegean, surrounded by the mainland on the north and west, by Asia Minor on the east, and studded by islands—483 by one count, though no more than one-tenth were ever significantly occupied—ranging down to the bulk of Crete on the south.[19] Ancient Hellas was only a geographical term, equivalent to the word "Europe" today; it was divided by water and mountains into many independent units, even though these shared from the Dark Ages just after 1000 B.C. onwards a common culture and language.

Always in the background of Greek life and thought lay the sea; early in the *Iliad* Odysseus and his crew "lifted the mast, and spread the white sails, the wind filled the great sail, the purple wave swished and poppled against the stern, the ship ran free on her way over the waters." But it was not always so favorable, "as the long billows roll to the shore line after line when the west wind drives: the swell gathers head far out on the sea, then bursts on the land in thunder, rearing and curving its crest about the headlands and spitting out the salt spray."[20] Even steamships can shudder and toss when the north wind whistles down the central Aegean, and ancient small sailing craft, like the modern caiques, put to sea only in good weather.

Nowhere in southern or central Greece are men more than 40 miles, a day or so on foot, from the sea;[21] nowhere in the Aegean, again, will a ship be entirely out of sight of land on a clear day, until it breaks out to the south beyond Crete and Rhodes into the eastern Mediterranean. These conditions encouraged seafaring from Paleolithic times onward—obsidian from the island of Melos has been found in Late Paleolithic contexts on the mainland. Yet when an ambassador to Athens told its assembly, "Most of you draw your subsistence from the sea," his statement could have been true only for an exceptional state in a developed economy. Hesiod asserted that he had once been to sea—to cross the 100-yard Euripus strait from Boeotia to Euboea!—and though giving advice about shipping seasons warned that "it is fearful to die among the waves."[22]

Among the major ancient states, Sparta and Thebes did not lie on the sea. Athens, Argos, and Corinth were some distance inland; it was primarily colonies which were sited directly on the coast. Thucydides surmised that the inland locations were caused by fear of naval raids, which took place from Minoan times onward;[23] Athenian external trade, however vigorous one conceives it to have been, passed over the open roadstead of Phalerum down to 500. If Themistocles soon thereafter began the fortification of the Piraeus, it was largely to protect the base of the first major Athenian naval building program. From Thucydides onward, there has been an unwarranted emphasis on sea power as the shaping force in ancient Greek history, partly as a reflection of an equally unjustified stress on English sea power in modern history; the major Greek state down to 500 was the land power Sparta, though, interestingly enough, it was more advanced in naval operations in the sixth century than was Athens.[24]

Most Greeks lived and died without ever going to sea, but those who did dare to sail abroad were to link the Aegean world with vital outside influences across prehistoric and historic times alike. Commercial activity by sea was channeled into the regions about the Saronic gulf and the gulf of Argos, between the rocky coasts of the Peloponnesus on the south and on the north the jagged mountains of Thessaly, a dangerous shore in all seasons; it was accordingly these central districts, less favored in climate, which were normally the leaders in native cultural progress.

Rise and Fall of the Early Aegean World

Down through the Slavic and Albanian infiltrations in relatively recent centuries, peoples have been able to move on foot into Greece, but as landsmen they have been slow to entrust themselves to the seas beyond. From the advanced ancient centers of civilization in the Near East, ideas and techniques reached the Aegean by perilous sea ventures along the southern coast of Asia

Minor, but their further transmission by land was checked or slowed by the ecological barrier between Greek evergreen scrub and Balkan deciduous forests. The Aegean, in other words, was in antiquity uniquely fortunate in opportunities for the fusion of peoples and ideas, and served as a cauldron or mixing pot for this process at least twice in its early history.

The second of these mergers, in the early centuries of the first millennium B.C., was the basic impetus for all the developments discussed in later pages; the first had less lasting consequences but is fascinating in its immediate effects. By 1600 the inhabitants of Crete had been fired by native evolution and foreign influence into the great glory of the developed Minoan civilization, centered in palaces such as those of Cnossus, Phaestus, Mallia, and others; real towns with commercial and industrial sectors arose about the palaces, and in public administration, writing in the Linear A script was used for inventories and other purposes.

On the mainland a paler imitation appeared in the hilltop fortresses of Mycenae and elsewhere, including palaces at Pylos, Athens, and as far north as Volos. Here too the native chieftains or *wanaktes* aped the developed states of the Near East by establishing a bureaucracy, the scribes of which wrote on clay tablets in the Linear B script; thanks to the ingenuity and protracted efforts of Michael Ventris and John Chadwick it is now clear that this was used to express Greek, in a syllabary of 89 signs. The contents of the tablets are inventories of sheep, weapons, and chariots, payments of copper to dependent smiths, and sacrifices to Athena, Dionysus, and other deities. True towns did not emerge about Mycenaean palaces, but the rural population was governed by headsmen called *basileis* on behalf of the powerful *wanaktes*.

The presence of Egyptians is suggested in Crete, and Mesopotamian seals have turned up in Thebes; on the whole, however, it was clearly Mycenaeans and, to a lesser extent, Minoans, who plied the seas. To the east, where they established posts on the east coast of the Aegean and in Cyprus, Aegean seafarers sought the luxuries manufactured in Egypt and Syria; to the west they traded with the natives of Italy and Sicily primarily for raw products, including metals, and probably for slaves as well. If one can rely at all on later legends, the masters of the palaces engaged in a great deal of internecine warfare and were not averse to looting and piracy on the seas; but as Braudel showed in his great work on the Mediterranean in the sixteenth century after Christ, piracy has always been an endemic curse of its waters.

In the closing stages of the Mycenaean age, the citadels at least of Mycenae and Athens were more heavily fortified, and secure approaches to water supplies were provided. Even so, Mycenaean civilization vanished from 1250 onward in a wave of sacking and burning of its palaces. Mycenae apparently was the last to fall, about 1150, and thereafter the Aegean was reduced to as low a level of life as it had experienced for over a millennium. The peasants in the villages round about the fortresses may have watched almost with joy as smoke spiraled up from the gleaming palaces, but they suffered too. Social, economic, and political organization swiftly sank, and with it fell the population; in many areas the lowlands seem to have been abandoned to nomads, and the few survivors often withdrew to mountain villages.[25]

All over the Levant the close of the Bronze Age brought catastrophe. In Asia Minor the Hittite realms disappeared as completely as did those of the Aegean; invaders attacked Egypt by land and sea in 1190–85 but were beaten back by Ramses III in great battles which he had depicted on his temple at Medinet Habu. Civilization also survived in Syria, though some of its cities were sacked and deserted and local kings no longer built palaces. Greek tradition remembered the coming of the Dorians, apparently located on the northwest fringe of Mycenaean lands; and the most economical explanation of the collapse—discounting the theory that natives rebelled against ruthless exploitation—still remains an invasion led by Dorian-speaking peoples. This wave settled throughout most of the Peloponnesus and, unlike many earlier incursions, pushed out across the southern islands, including Crete, as far as Halicarnassus and other Dorian states on the coast of Asia Minor. The direct effects were devastating; but in the long range the inhabitants of the Aegean, cut off from outside contacts, fashioned in the Dark Ages 1150–750 B.C. the framework of historical Greek civilization.

The emphasis in preceding pages on the cultural stimuli radiating out from the Near East may be misleading in one respect. Even today a visitor from North America or western Europe feels that he has passed a great divide when he enters Greek lands; and Greeks themselves will comment that they "are going to Europe," meaning Italy or France. Yet one need only plunge on farther to Cairo, Tehran, or even Istanbul to realize that Athens today is basically tied to western European culture. As Karamanlis proclaimed on signing the EEC treaty in 1979, "We have resolved that we will be all Europeans, as Churchill would say, and as Shelley would say, all Greeks. For in the words of Isocrates, Greeks are not those who were born in Greece but all those who have adopted the classical spirit." On the other hand, as this great statesman pointed out to Eisenhower 20 years earlier, Greece "belongs ideologically to the West, but she is isolated geographically and racially."[26]

To sum up the picture thus far, the Greeks of antiquity were primarily farmers living in tightly united families in villages; whether they cultivated the red soils of Attica or the purplish plains of Boeotia, agricultural techniques provided a relatively secure existence. Droughts could occur, and early Greek poetry knows of famines and plagues, which were usually explained as curses of the gods on unjust rulers; but such disasters were exceptions, not the rule. This landscape could not support the teeming masses of Mesopotamian cities or of the villages clustered along the Nile, nor would it in itself produce great riches concentrated in the hands of a dominant upper class. The famous wealthy Greeks of modern generations such as Averoff and Onassis gained their riches abroad in Egyptian cotton or world shipping, not from Greek fields; as the exiled Spartan king Demaratus told Xerxes, "Greece has always had poverty as her companion."[27] Priests and kings of the Near East used gold and silver goblets; Greeks had to be content with clay cups. Many ancient Greeks owned little or no land; the majority of farmers held four hectares or so; only a few could own larger domains—the biggest estate known in classical Athens reached only to 30 hectares.[28] Life in the ancient Near East was framed in terms of majestic, almost static empires; the simpler Aegean society was to thrust forward in the centuries after 1000 B.C. to create and elaborate a very different political system in which the values of Western civilization were first made explicit and conscious. Eventually Aristotle could sum up the product: "Man is by nature an animal intended to live in a *polis*."[29]

CHAPTER II

An Age of Chieftains

Before the destruction of the Mycenaean political system in the late second millennium B.C., powerful *wanaktes* inhabited palaces which were decorated with frescoes and filled with an abundance of pottery, ivory figurines, and other products of skillful artists; they administered their territories with the aid of a bureaucracy which committed relevant information to writing. By 750 B.C., on the other hand, the Homeric epics and the great Dipylon vases attest the existence of the famous outlook on life known as Hellenic, i.e., a man-centered, logical cast of mind seeking harmony and proportion. In keeping with this virtual revolution, which was to lead the Greeks to ever more remarkable progress, the *polis* was emerging out of a primitive form of political organization, far different from that of Mycenaean times.

How can a modern student safely make his way into the Dark Ages, 1150–750 B.C., which form the backdrop for this great change?[1] There had been a material deterioration at the close of the Bronze Age and a massive decline in inhabitation. The population of one settlement, Lefkandi, has recently been estimated at no more than 50 across the Dark Ages, even though it was "one of the most active, outward-looking and even prosperous communities" of the era.[2] Writing was unnecessary for agricultural or nomadic peoples. Until the last few years one could safely say that not one building of any consequence had been erected across the period, but the English excavations at Lefkandi have now found a structure of some size—presumably a shrine of a local hero—in which a man, woman, and chariot with horses had been buried in the tenth century B.C.[3] Only a very few houses of the era are known, and no complete villages; the historian is reduced to considering graves and cemeteries. Of these the most important has been that of the Kerameikos, outside the later Dipylon gate of Athens, for this has provided a consecutive series of burials all across the Dark Ages which permits the firm establishment of a ceramic yardstick. The earliest style is Protogeometric, and this is followed by the more extensively decorative Geometric stage. Some limited metalwork also appears, but in Protogeometric contexts there is scarcely enough gold to make a large modern wedding ring; only as one comes down into the ninth and eighth centuries does a wider variety of objects begin to show in the graves.

This testimony does illuminate the beginnings and early stages of the Hellenic spirit; the Greeks were creating a new form of thought of great potential, only dimly fertilized by Mycenaean inheritance and quite independent of any outside influence. The physical evidence, however, gives virtually no guidance to political evolution among the peoples of Greece. For this aspect one must turn to the Homeric epics and Hesiod's *Works and Days,* for these do throw light on the ultimate roots of the vehicles for public activity which were to be consolidated in the *polis.* Yet in the Dark Ages they existed only in embryo within a context of peoples led by chieftains. This stage, the age of heroes, must be examined with some care both to determine the origins of the *polis* and to establish how markedly different the political temper of the era was from that of historic Greece.

Tribes and Chieftains

First, a necessary word of warning about Homer. The epics under his name are the first, and also the greatest, monuments of Greek literature; in this respect and in many others they present problems which have been fiercely debated for almost two centuries and which still elicit strong disagreements. In recent years, nonetheless, there has been a growing consensus that the epics, in their final form, are to be dated to the eighth century, the *Iliad* coming about a generation before the *Odyssey;* Hesiod's poem is most properly placed about 700.[4] It has become clear that the epic poets created their tales out of an ancestral stock of stories in a stylized, artificial vocabulary and a poetic technique which reached back centuries in oral transmission.

One must always keep in mind that the objective of these bards was not to write history but to explore human capabilities and limitations. In the *Iliad* the framework of the tale is a purported war against Troy. Whether that excursion of the well-greaved Achaeans ever took place is endlessly, and needlessly, debated; and efforts to find Mycenaean aspects reflected in any important respect in the epics must be thwarted by the gulf that separates the Mycenaean *wanaktes* and the Homeric *basileis*. Homer knew there had been an age of heroes when Hector lifted a stone which now two men could barely lift, but unlike Hesiod he did not view his own age as in any way one of decline. Rather the *Iliad* revolves about the emotional suffering of Achilles who must endure the death of his best friend, and, as counterpoint, the hopeless resignation of his great opponent, Trojan Hector, who must fall in revenge. In the *Odyssey* the long-enduring, wily hero Odysseus wanders across lands and seas of phantasmagoria, which cannot be equated with the real shores of the Mediterranean.

Nor is the picture of "Homeric society" fully consonant with any one point in the Dark Ages; a poet dependent on an inherited matrix "can select, he can conflate, he can idealise."[5] Yet a reasonably consistent picture of the patterns of political decisions can be drawn from the epics.

The leader in the Homeric world is the *basileus*, a term normally translated as "king" but more properly defined as "chieftain." Modern anthropological theory postulates that logically the earliest form of human organization is that of a tribe marked by an "egalitarian economy, with relatively simple tools to produce and primary goods to consume"; in this system the leaders are "unable to raise their own standards of living with the materials available."[6] As early as the archeological period known as Early Helladic (before 2000 B.C.), the Aegean had moved beyond this level to the stage of chieftains, one of whom occupied the House of the Tiles at Lerna near Argos; after the Mycenaean debacle chieftains again became dominant.

In a society of this type the tribesmen provide resources by which the leaders can live more abundantly in terms of food, equipment, and often housing; yet the chiefs of Polynesia are "morally obliged to be generous," to provide "entertainments for visiting dignitaries" and to succor the local people in times of need. "Where kinship is king, the king is in the last analysis only kinsman, and something less than royal. The same bonds that link a chief to the underlying population and give him his authority in the end tie his hands."[7] Other anthropologists, to be sure, minimize this role of collecting and redistributing resources and find "the primary role of the chief is to process information and manage interaction between communities."[8] In either case the power of a chieftain rests not on formal rules but on personality, and ultimately on his utility to his followers.

Let me note clearly that throughout later pages anthropological theories will be cited only as raising questions which may help in interpreting the ancient evidence; they cannot in themselves *prove* anything about Greek history. But the picture just suggested does provide useful parallels to the pattern of action in the *Iliad* and then to the testimony of change in the *Odyssey* and in Hesiod.

Political Procedures in the *Iliad*

There are actually two major examples in Greek literature of masses of warriors in the field who must take military decisions akin to political processes. In 401 B.C. Cyrus the Younger, brother of the Persian king, recruited some 10,000 Greek mercenaries and marched inland to wrest the throne from Artaxerxes. His troops won the battle of Cunaxa, but Cyrus himself was killed; thereafter the perfidious Persians managed to seize the generals of the Greek mercenaries. But the troops proceeded that night to select new generals, one of them the gentleman-venturer Xenophon, who wrote a magnificent tale, the *Anabasis,* of their march across the mountains of Asia Minor to the Black Sea. As they proceeded they resembled a moving *polis;* for the most part, the council of generals determined the next step, but at critical turning points, an assembly of all the men logically debated the problems and reached agreement by a show of hands, much as citizens operated in contemporary *poleis*.

Procedures in the *Iliad* were far less consciously structured.[9] At the very beginning of the epic, Homer makes clear that his subject is one of quarrel between two great heroes, Achilles and Agamemnon, and the evil effects to the Achaean host of the anger of Achilles.[10] The stage requires an audience, provided by the other heroes and the *laos* or mass of the Achaeans, who meet in a group usually entitled *agora;* later in the first two books other assemblies, both of Achaeans and Trojans and of the Olympian gods, are convoked for the purpose of information or of announcing decisions before warfare resumes.

In the first assembly Agamemnon accepts the necessity of ending Apollo's plague by returning the captive of war, Chryseis, to her father: "I would rather have the people alive than dead" (1. 117), but then he demands a prize in return. Like Zeus on Olympus (1. 581) he is a figure to be feared; Calchas the seer dares to announce the anger of Apollo only if protected by the oath of Achilles: "A *basileus* when angry can always be stronger than a common man" (1. 80). Yet it is not Agamemnon but Achilles who summons the *laos* and opens the meeting by stating its purpose.

An extended assembly is reported later in Book 19. Achilles himself goes along the ranks of the Achaeans calling all of them together; even the pilots and stewards who deal out food attend. His aim is to announce that he will rejoin battle and give over his rage against Agamemnon. The heroes Diomedes and Odysseus arrive, limping from wounds, and sit down in their appropriate places at the front of the gathering. Agamemnon comes last, and after Achilles speaks he answers "from the place where he was sitting, without coming forward to the front" as was customary. Agamemnon seeks to exculpate himself as misled by Ate and promises rich presents to Achilles as before. Achilles does not wish to delay but to resume battle. Odysseus objects that one must eat first and that the gifts should be displayed. Achilles again scorns the delay; when Odysseus stubbornly insists on eating before fighting, Achilles himself hastily dismisses the assembly.[11]

Elders appear at various points in the *Iliad,* as on the shield of

Achilles, but only once does a council (*boule*) of elders (2. 55ff.) convene before the *laos* meet, though one may feel that Agamemnon would have been advised to convoke it more frequently. At this council of sceptered *basileis,* "the great-souled elders," Agamemnon announces that he has had a dream from Zeus promising that he will take Troy, but that to the *laos* he will argue giving up the war. Nestor, *princeps senatus,* answers in approval, and all agree that the heralds shall assemble the people. When it comes together, the racket is terrific until more heralds quiet it down. There is no formal agenda or prayer to open the session; only *basileis* may properly speak and in doing so take hold of a scepter—as Polydamas informs Hector on another occasion, "No man of the *demos* is allowed to disagree by any means in council or in war" (12. 211ff.)—but as in the first meeting the leaders may blaze forth in rough, open anger, like that of children.[12]

Dissent is not impossible, but rarely are there two speakers in opposition or debate, as in the opening assembly or in a later meeting of the Trojan elders on the question of returning Helen to the Achaeans (7. 345ff.); in such disagreements only a higher power can adjudicate the issue—Athena in the slanging match of Achilles and Agamemnon, Priam in the later case. The auditors "vote" by shouting approval; by laughing at Odysseus' rebuke to the forward commoner Thersites, who is even beaten in public; or with their feet when encouraged to give up the war, militarily a foolish idea even if dramatically necessary.[13] Sometimes an elder statesman such as Nestor proposes a solution to the problem, and the assembly promptly dissolves. To emphasize a basic point: meetings of the assembly are not structured and are not primarily for the purpose of themselves making decisions; more often they convey information—a prime function of chieftains in the view of some anthropologists, as already noted. A remarkably close parallel to these procedures has been described among the Tswana of Bechuanaland.[14]

Major institutions of later Greek political organization—such as assembly and council—are present in the *Iliad;* what is missing? Basically, the lack of order and regular procedure; and the location of ultimate decision in the hands of an assembly of citizens. To draw a parallel from contemporaneous art which may be useful, the greatest masterpieces of Geometric pottery are the huge Dipylon craters and amphoras made in the eighth century to decorate graves in the Kerameikos. Like the *Iliad* itself, in which the metrical line has only 16 variants, these vases display a marvelous ability to create a complex structure out of a limited array of motifs, ordered by a sense of harmony and proportion; but the order is more instinctively than deliberately planned, as was to be the case in an Athenian red-figure vase of the fifth century.

The Power of the *Basileus*

In the *Iliad* the *basileus* is dominant and must protect the *laos*. "His cares are so many" (2. 24–25), yet it is equally clear that "we can't all be kings. Too many kings spoil a people. One king's enough for me, and why? He gets the right from Zeus on high" (2. 203–6). Again, "greater honor belongs to a sceptred king, when Zeus has given him dignity" (1. 279).

So it is Agamemnon above all who is given the title of *anax andron* (2. 402, 5. 38, 6. 33) while Achilles usually is only "leader of men" (6. 99).[15] On the field of battle Agamemnon commonly gives the orders, though heralds of the Achaeans and Trojans decide when it is time to stop fighting; he can command death for the skulker.[16] Priam picks him out amid the Achaean host as valiant and tall: "So fine a man I never did see, or so royal. He is every inch a king" (3. 167ff).

Yet his position has its ambiguities. Helen goes on to identify Odysseus and Ajax as worthy of esteem. Achilles can call the *laos* together on his authority and roundly assails Agamemnon as a "folk-devouring *basileus*" (1. 231); Diomedes refuses the idea of fleeing from the war when Agamemnon suggests it and proclaims that he will remain alone if necessary (9. 32ff.). Agamemnon, brave in battle and the ostensible leader, in fact has feet of clay. He is changeful, easily despairing, poor in judgment with regard to Achilles (whence Poseidon bluntly speak in the midst of the battle among the ships, "all because of an incompetent leader and slack followers" 13. 108). And the second time Agamemnon proposes flight, Odysseus frankly tells him, "Let no

other Achaean hear these words which no man ought to let pass
his lips, if he knows what decent talk is like, much less a sceptred
king; what you said just now seems to me simple nonsense" (14.
83ff.). It takes Nestor, Odysseus, Diomedes, and Menelaus to keep
him upright and on the proper path.

Zeus, on the other hand, is not to be countered; even his own
brother Poseidon must slink about to oppose his orders, partly by
getting Hera to lull Zeus to sleep. The world of the undying gods
is perfect; the human world is not so even on the level of the
sceptered *basileis,* whose power rests not on rules but on persuasive abilities and personal loyalty. Their functions are limited to
leadership in war, which at this period involves mainly border-
raiding to seize cattle, women, and other moveables; to sacrifices
to the gods; to protection of justice, though on the shield of
Achilles a law suit is actually settled by village elders; and to
lavish hospitality to foreigners and followers.[17]

The latter aspect is one, it will be remembered, which is prominent among the chieftains of Polynesia. In the *Iliad* Nestor at
one point urges Agamemnon, "You are the paramount *basileus.*
Call the elder men to dine; that is right and proper for you.
There is plenty of wine in your stores, which comes every day in
our ships over the sea from Thrace; all entertainment is yours,
and your subjects are many" (9. 70ff.). Agamemnon must promise
Achilles tripods, gold cauldrons, horses, women, booty of Troy,
his own daughter; and as a clincher Agamemnon exclaims:
"Seven flourishing cities I will give to him . . . in them inhabit
men rich in flocks and rich in cattle, who shall worship him with
their tribute and obey his judgments under his sceptre" (9. 122ff.).
Equally open-handed is Achilles in his provision of prizes at the
funeral games for Patroclus, including a lump of iron so large a
man will not have to go to a neighboring *polis* to gain the metal
for his shepherd or ploughman (23. 831ff.).

As has been observed, this prodigality accords poorly with the
conditions of the Dark Ages, and it is far from clear how Agamemnon and Achilles have acquired such wealth.[18] In the world
of the *Iliad* there are no taxes, and as Achilles points out, the
Achaean host has "no wealth laid up in common store" (1. 124).[19]
When the Trojans plan to offer half their possessions to Achilles,

it is the elders, not Priam, who so decide (22. 119). A *basileus* has
his own estate or *temenos* (18. 550ff.) and can own 300 horses
(20. 221); but Homer feels no need to explain how the "stewards
of the people" pay for their imports of grain and wine. One can
only surmise that the logistical infrastructure of the invaders was
based on the fruits of raids.

Always beside the *basileus,* however, are the people, the *laos*
or *demos*.[20] They are inferior in beauty, at least in the case of the
unfortunate Thersites, and they can be treated contemptuously;
in assembling the Achaeans Odysseus courteously invites leaders
but men of the *demos* he strikes and tells to be quiet (2. 200ff.).
At Troy the assembly seems to be composed of two elements, the
young and the elders (2. 789); the Achaeans are organized in
tribes and phratries (2. 362). In battle they march silently in
"dark battalions, bristling with shields and spears" (4. 281–82),
and close formations recur repeatedly on the battlefield; one may
suspect that the dramatic requirements of the plot led Homer to
emphasize unduly the role of individual duels.[21] Generally the
poet has no place for the ordinary man, though in a simile he
draws a comparison with a woman spinning "that she may win a
meager wage for her children" (12. 435).[22] Yet the *laos* is never
pictured as a cowed, helpless mass; leaders must have followers.

The other "political" term in the *Iliad* is the word *polis* itself.
Trojan allies are directly listed as coming from *poleis* (2. 806ff.);
in the Achaean catalogue the groupings are often wider than in
the historical geography of the *polis* world.[23] The word has
varied shades of meaning. At times, as on the shield of Achilles
(18. 490ff.), it is an inhabited site, sometimes with walls, which is
often translated as "city"; but the Dark Ages lacked true cities in
the historical sense of centers possessing significant commercial
and industrial sections, and urban walls appear as a rule only in
the colonies down into classical times; the Homeric *polis* rather
is a rural agglomeration with at most a few smiths and potters.
Elsewhere *polis* seems an equivalent for homeland; in the *Odyssey* the usual question of strangers is, "What is your *polis* and
your parents?"[24] but nowhere does it have the defined meaning
of later days as an organized "state." The political world of the
Iliad is still lacking in clearly marshalled order.

The Beginnings of Change: The *Odyssey* and Hesiod

The *Odyssey* is a much weaker epic than the *Iliad;* its author
wrestles, not always successfully, with the problem of following
now the trials of Odysseus and then the travels of his son Telemachus. There is also too much repetition, and the drive of the
plot is less forceful. In many ways it hints at changes in divers
fields, though one must always recall that any one passage in the
Odyssey may be as ancient as anything in the *Iliad.*

Especially interesting is the description of the land of the
Cyclops, to which Odysseus comes after visiting the Lotus Eaters,
for in this legendary world the inhabitants lack the characteristics of life which an epic audience considered proper. Thus they
are overweening and lawless (9. 106ff.), without assemblies to give
council and proper ordinances; each one sets rules for his children and wives, and pays no attention to the rights of the community. The Cyclops also lack ships and shipwrights so that they
do not visit their neighbors; Polyphemus in particular knows
nothing of justice (*dike*) or law (*themistas*). When Odysseus emphasizes that Zeus avenges suppliants and strangers, Polyphemus
abruptly dismisses any fear of the gods. The differences from
Greek conventional views are evident; Aristotle's opinion was
that anyone outside a political community must be either a god
or a hunted animal.[25] Yet unlike many societies, where the
stranger is suspect or even rejected, ancient Greeks were on the
whole willing to receive foreigners (*xenoi*), especially aristocrats,
who might have local ties, but also craftsmen and even exiles;
Zeus encouraged friendly reception of *xenoi.*[26]

In the *Odyssey* the *basileus* continues to be pictured as master:
"Do you think it the worst thing in the world to be a *basileus?*
It is not a bad thing at all. He gets plenty of wealth, he is highly
honored" (1. 391–93). Alcinous is respected as if a god (7. 11) and
his wife as a goddess (7. 71). Later when the suitors of Penelope
consider removing Telemachus, one of them observes that "it is
a dread thing to kill one of a princely race" (16. 401–2). Yet the
duty of the *basileus* to provide due process is far more clearly
emphasized than in the *Iliad;* and in the *Odyssey* the gods more

often and more directly demand proper action; "the poem as a whole becomes a moral paradigm."[27]

Hesiod went further in stressing the role of the Olympians in settling disputes among men and securing punishments. He himself had suffered injustice in the decisions of his native "bribe-swallowing *basileis*" to award most of his father's land to his iniquitous brother Perses; but his poem advances swiftly from the specific event to a general portrayal of Zeus as aided by 30,000 watchers of mortal men with regard to their judgments and wrong deeds; virgin Dike sits by his side. "Where there are those who devour bribes and give sentence with crooked judgments," Zeus punishes with famine, plague, a lack of children, and destruction at home and on the sea; those who give straight judgments to strangers and natives have peace, no war, famine or disaster, and good food: "Their women bear children like their parents. They do not travel on ships."[28] Much the same picture of the proper *basileus,* setting the people aright if misguided in assembly, occurs in the other poem assigned to Hesiod, the *Theogony* (80ff., 434ff.). In both the *Odyssey* and in Hesiod's works the responsibility for justice is in the hands of Zeus, watching over the *basileus;* there is not yet any idea that men by their own actions can secure or restore justice to a community.

More directly political is the emphasis in the *Odyssey* on precise order and rules, reflected in the contempt for the ways of the Cyclops and in the description of the land of the Phaeacians, a new settlement which almost resembles a Greek colony with its harbor, division of rural lands, and public areas (6. 9ff.). Alcinous is *basileus,* but he has a formal council of 12 other *basileis;* at one point he proposes that they give Odysseus the conventional tokens of wealth, tripods and cauldrons, and recoup their costs by what amounts to a tax or *eisphora* on the citizenry as a whole (13. 14–15). Public (*demosios*) and private are often distinguished (3. 82, 4. 314).

Meetings of citizens now take place in a special area, also called *agora,* fitted with polished stones. The assembly is described as "many voiced" (2. 150); elsewhere a time is given as "the hour when a man rises from the assembly for his supper, one that decides the many quarrels of young men that seek a judgment" (12. 439–40). In another passage Nestor looks back to the Trojan war and tells Telemachus that he and Odysseus always voiced the same views in the *agora* and in the *boule,* but unanimity was not universal; Nestor mentions an assembly of the Achaeans called by Menelaus and Agamemnon, "quite wrong, most improper, at sunset of all times" (3. 138). The two brothers disagreed, and the Achaeans, heavy with wine, split into two parties as to whether to abandon the war at once or first to sacrifice. Such a division of the *laos* never appears in the *Iliad,* nor is there this emphasis on the need for orderly procedures.

Because the scene of the *Odyssey* is not a battlefield but at times the island of Ithaca, the general mass of its inhabitants occasionally is visible; the suitors of Penelope fear that the populace may cause them trouble (16. 375, 425). Class division is also more pronounced; slaves appear as well as beggars—one of whom is described as a "public beggar" (18. 1)—and vagabond folk who sleep in the smithy or *lesche* (18. 328–29). The distinction between sceptered *basileis* and base churls (*kakoi*) is stressed in 4. 62–64, though these lines are often considered by ancient and modern scholars retrojection from a later age.[29] In the underworld Achilles tells Odysseus that he would rather be a *thes* in life, a man without a *kleros,* whose livelihood is but small (11. 489–90)—a lot which is clearly intended to represent the bottom of the economic and social scale. The *demos* is differentiated: *demioergoi,* workers for the community such as prophets, healers of illness, builders, and divine minstrels, who "are bidden all over the boundless earth," appear in 17. 383ff.

In the *Odyssey,* thus, society is portrayed as complicated and even to some degree stratified, but one must not build too much on this. A recent effort to show that the poet was often reacting to social upheavals and economic distress among the peasants and was "openly hostile in his full scathingly unsympathetic portrait of [the suitors'] naive and arrogant disregard for the self-respect of less fortunate men" is anachronistic, to say the least, and fails to take into account the dramatic necessity of picturing the suitors in a black light.[30] Even so, while the Homeric epics are similar in vocabulary and technique, changes in many aspects of life are apparent in the *Odyssey;* this political, social, and cultural evolution will be further treated in the next chapter in the discussion of the physical evidence of the eighth century.

Social Structure and Values

Like the tragedians of classical Athens the epic poets necessarily concentrated on the deeds and misfortunes of great men, and so depicted mainly personalities, emancipated heroes who dared much even if they must pay a price for their self-assertion. Since the *Iliad* in particular remained the one book which all Greeks were most likely to know, this outlook was a leaven in later Hellenic history, but certainly there was little scope for the individual in village life during the Dark Ages.[31] To comprehend fully the matrix out of which the *polis* was to emerge, one must keep in mind the enduring influence of early social organization.

Homer, to be sure, had no reason to provide us with a tidy blueprint of this structure; for guidance one must rely on survivals of the customs of a preliterate age into a later era of written materials, but Greek life was so rurally based at the outset that one can assume with some confidence basic continuities. In looking at attitudes and values animating day-to-day life during the Dark Ages, however, the historian must tread his way carefully, for modern theories have often been utilized to supplement or clarify obscure areas. Even where a view so based has become standard, we must not hesitate to reject it if it is contradicted by the ancient evidence.

Beside the community as a whole, the tribe or *ethnos,* "there was only the *oikos,*" the basic structure for ensuring the survival of a society, the building block with which Aristotle began his analysis in the *Politics.*[32] The word is normally translated as "family," a pale term which scarcely suggests its powerful bonds. Loyalty to "the dear fatherland" is an evident force in both *Iliad* and *Odyssey,* but wherever this encouragement to bravery is stated more precisely, it commonly becomes one's father, wife and children, and estates.[33] The *oikos* thus embraced both the biological family and animals, slaves, retainers—though these are visible mainly in domestic service and are not numerous even in attendance on the Olympian gods[34]—and above all the plot of land, the *kleros,* which guaranteed economic independence and political standing.

Efforts, however, to show that land was communally owned or at least could not be alienated at this time cannot be upheld against the factual testimony of the epics, Hesiod, and other early examples of the transfer or even sale of land.[35] True, possession of a *kleros* was a vital part of "freedom" and was not lightly yielded. Care was taken down into historical times to see that *epikleroi,* heiresses, who were not uncommon in an era of high mortality, married relatives so that in some sense land was the property of a social unit rather than of an individual person. Common land or *eschatia* did exist on the fringes of cultivated areas, but this could be brought into personal ownership by eager men, grubbing out the brush and heaping up mounds of stone, a process visible in eighth-century Attica and elsewhere. In view of the average age of death, a son could normally expect to inherit his plot quite early.

Masculine dominance is obvious wherever one looks at the Dark Ages, whether in the epics or in the clay and bronze fig- urines of the era, almost always of warriors and their horses. At Troy the Achaeans were formally grouped in phratries; such brotherhoods remained powerful social units into historic times, a base for the reorganization of Spartan life in the sixth century and even at Athens the primary unit for determining citizenship. These groups often assembled for common meals (*syssitia*) and drinking bouts (*symposia*), at which the epic bards recited their tales of great heroes; in these meetings much public business must have been decided informally without any need for public ratification.[36]

Valiant attempts have been made in recent generations to dis- cover a matriarchal structure in the earliest days of Aegean his- tory, partly because Marxist thought has taken up the theories of Bachofen to reenforce its idyllic picture of primeval lack of class or sex exploitation. This view has never been able to mar- shal adequate evidence, and most certainly does not reflect Greek life from the Dark Ages onward. Agamemnon condemns the entire race of women (especially Clytemnestra), and common women are portrayed wrangling in the village street "with words true and false,"[37] though in the *Odyssey* there is frequent praise of women. Hesiod is a calculating man: "Do not let a flaunting woman coax and deceive you; she is after your barn. The man who trusts womankind trusts deceivers" (*Works and Days* 373–75). In subsequent poets of the archaic age, womankind is both necessary to man and a curse, dangerous in its irrationality and credulity. The son must fight, in Aeschylus' words, "for the ashes of his father"; the problem for Orestes is that he must avenge his father's murder even if this forces him to execute his mother. There was accordingly little likelihood that women would ever enjoy public political rights, though below the surface a strong-minded wife might well dominate her family.[38]

In every discussion of early Greek society down to the present day, the clan or *genos* is presented as a major grouping of families, especially on the upper-class level. Belief in the presence of this institution in Greek life owes much to the models provided by Roman *gentes* (it is always dangerous, though, to transfer concepts from Rome to Greece), Scotch clans, and anthropological parallels; but the *genos* must now disappear. In a lengthy, well-buttressed dissertation Bourriot has demolished it as essentially a modern fabrication and has shown that the only true *gene* were the royal clans of Sparta and some priestly clans here and there, as at Eleusis.[39]

The public role of kinship, indeed, has been much exaggerated, following the famous but no longer fully accepted picture by Maine of transition from kinship to territoriality as a mark of political advance and the treatments of modern primitive tribes of Polynesia and Africa, often with elaborate charts or descriptions of who may marry whom. As Finley observed in a well-known book on the Dark Ages, for Radcliffe-Brown "the conduct of individuals to one another is very largely regulated on the basis of kinship" and goes on to comment that "this is no description of the world of Odysseus, in which the family tie, though strong, was narrowly defined," and the personal ties of leader and follower were a far more powerful cement.[40] Hesiod only once mentions kinsmen, likely to be slow to react whereas neighbors will bring rapid aid in an emergency, and describes agricultural life largely in terms of relations to one's neighbors. His advice in marriage seems to be totally oblivious to kinship; a man should marry a maiden who is much younger. "For a man wins nothing better than a good wife," and nothing worse than a bad one "who roasts her man without fire."[41] Kinship always remained a force on the personal level in exacting vengeance or blood-money for a murder, but it cannot be used, as it has been too often, to explain political groupings and activities, even in the Dark Ages, much less in classical Athens. Far more influential were the links to neighbors by tight, almost unconscious bonds, including religious ceremonies at local shrines and the multifold ties of village life.

In assessing the values dominant in this world, one must turn back to the epics, but in doing so must be careful not to describe Homeric heroes as aristocrats. They were indeed distinguished in birth as Zeus-sprung or as the scions of great fathers; they were frequently given the title of *basileus;* their roles as leaders were deliberately emphasized. In public life they sought *arete* or reputation; booty and wealth were cherished particularly as reinforcing popular esteem. Men and women of this stamp are described in the *Odyssey* as being more delicate and beautiful than the ordinary people. "Our delight is in feasting, in music, and dancing, plenty of clean linen, a warm bath, and bed" (8. 248, 13. 223).

All this sounds very much like the ways of life of the upper classes in early modern Europe; a recent survey of Greek ethics points out that in the Homeric world those who were best were warriors, men of wealth and social position who protected their dependents by their valor in war and peace, and concludes, "This is an aristocratic scale of values."[42] The statements are correct; the inference is premature. The Homeric world had not yet traveled all the way toward the elaboration of a true aristocratic ethos, i.e., an obligatory pattern of life and values *consciously* conceived and shared by a limited group which inherited its belief that it was "best" and whose claims were generally accepted, even cherished, by other groups of society.[43]

This is not a minor point; rather, the judgment is a vital one in assessing the lines of development out of the Dark Ages. For the view that Homeric heroes were at most precursors of the aristocrats of historic Greece, one can marshal a variety of evidence. Physical work, for example, was not disdained; in peacetime, Paris tended sheep on Mount Ida and Odysseus plowed the fields of his native Ithaca. Skill in crafts is also praised both for men and for gods, as for Hephaestus in his smithy. Only in later centuries was emphasis on leisure to become a prime requisite of aristocratic life. Down into modern times aristocrats have been born such, not made; and even if scions of noble ancestors who are themselves without wit can be scorned, there has always been an underlying assumption that inheritance is the first, decisive step toward *arete*.[44] Despite their Zeus-sprung origins, on the other hand, Homeric heroes had to gain their own distinction by personal skill either in battle or in the *agora*. Both Achilles and Hector ruefully admit that they excel only on the field of war whereas Odysseus is deft in both,[45] and in *Odyssey* 8. 157ff. the proper conclusion is drawn that men are of varied talents and so need each other.

In recent years the conventional view of the economic interests of these heroes has limited their patterns of exchange of property to pure gift-giving, an interpretation which owes much to the influential essay by Marcel Mauss, *Essai sur le Don*.[46] This is too narrow a picture. Leaders in many ages, to be sure, have practiced gift exchange; but not all men are leaders, ostensibly disinterested in gain, and even those who are privileged usually have a real sense of relative values. In the one example of exchange in the *Iliad* the audience may be imagined as smiling grimly when Homer pointed out that Glaucus traded with Diomedes gilded armor for bronze, "the price of a hundred oxen for nine" (6. 236). Aristocrats—and commoners as well—trade presents on festive occasions or to satisfy ceremonial needs with visitors, but not all transfer of property is necessarily so motivated. A recent discussion of early Greece distinguishes between luxuries, given on the upper levels of society, and a "substantive" array of food and other items used by all classes and concludes that by 700 a more truly economic system had emerged.[47] Not only in exchange but in other areas as well there are hints of a more complicated economic pattern than is sometimes noticed. Labor for hire, for instance, appears in the simile of a poor woman who earns a wage by spinning, but gods as well expect recompense for labor, as did Poseidon and Apollo in building the walls of Troy (though they did not get their wages).[48] Even the term "profit" (*kerdos*) appears in the *Odyssey* when Odysseus pretends to be a trader. Life in the villages of the Dark Ages was still largely traditional, but the winds of change were beginning to blow.

To sum up, a rigid stratification in which the upper classes were truly aristocratic in ways of life, economic attitudes, and emphasis on kinship did not yet exist in the dim centuries before 700. Rather, the communities of the Greek landscape must be seen as possessing a fundamental unity; Nester in the *Iliad* says that "a man without phratry, law or hearth is he who is in love with civil war, that brutal, ferocious thing."[49] One cannot hope to understand how the *polis* emerged and survived the tensions of the age of expansion after 750 if the social system was divided from the beginning.

A last aspect of early Greek society needs brief comment. Even in historical times what one can only call superstition continued to produce rituals for the phenomena of menstruation, childbirth, and other upsetting aspects of physical life.[50] Whereas magic is remarkably absent in the epics, Hesiod gives directions to avoid cutting one's nails with iron tools and orders the blessing of pots by the village sorcerer. The Greeks were as primitive in the Dark Ages as any people studied by modern anthropologists; the important fact is that they did not in the end allow their life to be fettered by taboos and other rigid prescriptions. As they moved into a historical era in which literature and the arts evolved continuously toward the magnificent products of the classical era they dragged with them much of this ancestral inheritance: "Greek cities in their highest prosperity still retained many of the usages peculiar to the tribal communities from which they had sprung."[51]

This chapter has revealed a fundamental ambiguity. On the one side stand the Homeric heroes, subject only to the will of the gods and even then at times with reluctance; on the other the society of the era could allow almost no independent place to its individual members, whether leaders or followers. This division was to continue across succeeding centuries and was to produce serious frictions when a true aristocracy appeared, but in the end the dichotomy gave way to an essential harmony. Even though the epics became canonical and gave inspiration to art, religion, and literature, the way of life of the upper classes was to be refined beyond the raw self-assertion of Homeric heroes and so eventually was tempered. The rigidities of conformity were also to yield as economic and social advance permitted more flexibility, a development which required a long period of evolution.

CHAPTER III

Crystallization of the *Polis*

As the eighth century drew toward its close, the texture of Hellenic civilization became more varied. Abroad, the Greeks were now in continuous contact with the Near Eastern centers of advanced technology; in western waters they founded colony after colony on the shores of Italy and Sicily. The first temples appeared; the makers of bronze and clay figurines grew venturesome, though their nude male representations were still conceived as an assembly of parts rather than as an integrated whole. Both the shapes and the decoration of vases changed remarkably; the formal designs of the Dipylon amphoras and craters yielded in the generation from 735 to 680 at Corinth to freehand drawing, a style badly misnamed Orientalizing inasmuch as it owed nothing to the Near East in its fundamental characteristics. These Protocorinthian vases also utilized, for the first time, though only occasionally, scenes from myth and heroic legend. By the end of the century Hesiod had systematized, though not criticized, traditional views of the origin of the world and of man in the *Theogony*. This was an age of beginnings rather than of completions.

The concept of Zeitgeist, a common spirit infusing all aspects of culture in an era, is a very attractive one to the historian, and in later pages parallels between artistic and literary changes and political developments will be discussed. Yet the concept can lead one to create false similarities and to accept naive modes of explanation. Poets and poems do not themselves produce political activity, though ancient poets were highly regarded as halting civil strife and encouraging public unity, voices of the community as well as expressing their own emotions;[1] but they reflect very well the environment in which those changes could occur. The great political alteration, of course, was the emergence of the *polis,* an unprecedented form of organization of mankind.

Appearance of the *Polis*

In the epics the Zeus-sprung *basileis* occupy the center of the stage, not only in the poetic action but as leaders in an almost static tribal system. By the classical period, on the other hand, the firmly organized *polis* structure of public life is dominant in Athens, Corinth, Sparta, and other states. There were, indeed, still "backward" Greeks grouped in tribal systems, but they did not furnish the motive forces of Hellenic history.

The *polis* can be traced back across the sixth and even seventh centuries. In the Homeric Hymn to Apollo, in which Leto wanders about the Aegean, seeking a place to give birth to her son, states are named, not peoples.[2] But then the literary evidence halts, save for Hesiod and the Homeric epics, and in these the *polis* as known in historical days does not yet exist. The vital changes thus took place in an era so dark that conclusions both about the date and about the geographical area in which the *polis* emerged must always remain tentative.

There are still efforts to locate the origins of the *polis* in Ionia, partly because Old Smyrna had been a walled nucleus by the ninth century; but Greek settlements on alien shores might well require such protection, and in any case the *polis* must always be approached as a psychological and spiritual, not physical bond. Moreover, the earlier tendencies to overstress the creative role of the Asiatic seaboard in Greek history are now largely discounted.[3] The earliest true wars of which there was any memory took place in the southern part of the mainland; and if war be, in Clausewitz' words, "an act of force to compel our enemy to do our will," the political units involved must have been able to form and execute deliberate intentions which ran far beyond Homeric cattle-reeving.[4]

These wars also are relevant to the question of the date of the emergence of the *polis,* for they fall in the years just before 700.

Other evidence pointing to the same chronological era is provided by colonization. Although the earliest Greek post thus far known in the west, that at Pithecusae on the island of Ischia, might well have been the center for individual traders to Etruscan markets and metal workers using the iron ores of the mainland, it is difficult to see how the succeeding colonies such as Cumae and Syracuse, from about 750, which were deliberately established as agricultural settlements in which each member had his own plot of land, could have been undertaken or have sunk lasting roots unless the participants were united in a firm political system, i.e., a *polis*. On the whole the safest date for its appearance must be about the middle of the eighth century.[5] The reasons for describing the process as "crystallization" may be reserved for the close of this chapter; first one needs to determine what kind of institution one is seeking to find and by what lines of approach its presence can be detected.

There are in history concepts so familiar that it is easily assumed everyone knows their meaning. The *polis* is such an important concept in Greek history and civilization that no student of Hellenic development can fail to bring it into his discussion—but almost always he does so without any very serious effort at definition beyond, perhaps, the equation "small city-state." Small the *polis* was, but Greece had no true cities with specialized economic sectors until about 600; in a famous statement Thucydides observed that even in his own day the center of Sparta was no more than a cluster of four villages, though no one would deny that it was a *polis*. As for the second noun in the usual English rendering, one cannot avoid the term "state" in a political analysis, but the *polis* differed fundamentally from the abstract entity implied in that word as used from Machiavelli onward.[6]

In Homer the term *polis* denotes an agglomeration of people, sometimes fortified, or a person's homeland, but does not directly have a political significance. From the eighth century on it does have that meaning, a state marked by regular rules of procedure and a structure by which its citizens (however defined and limited) could establish and administer those rules; in the *polis,* moreover, all major activity was conducted at one specific spot not by bureaucrats but by the citizens themselves.[7] As a consequence of this second characteristic, the *polis* was initially and always remained a small area with clear boundaries, often natural in the form of mountains and seas; but since it emerged in a period in which the tribes or *ethne* were home-keeping peoples, it would in any case have been minuscule. That it continued to be so was a reflection of the spiritual and religious unity of its inhabitants, which was an essential quality. As Alcaeus put it, "Not stone and timber make . . . *poleis;* but wheresover are men who know how to keep themselves safe there are walls and there *poleis.*"[8] In another famous example, the wrangling council of generals at Salamis in 480 was divided as to whether to try again a naval battle with the Persians. When Themistocles urged the effort, the Corinthian Adeimantus bade him to be silent "because he was a man without a country"—Athens having been evacuated by its citizens. In rejoinder Themistocles pointed out that the Athenians still existed, and could found a new state in Italy if need be. In treaties it is the Athenians and the Lacedaemonians who contract terms, not territorial units. The *polis,* in sum, was "both more and less than a state, rather a human community, often very small indeed, always held together by narrow space, by religion, by pride, by life."[9]

The Physical Evidence

The vital question still remains: how and why did the Greeks shift from *ethnos* to *polis* in the more advanced areas? So great a step forward is not easily explained; in seeking an answer one must consider a variety of changes, but may hope in the end to formulate a reasonable view of the varied forces which conjoined felicitously to produce the *polis*. As always in early Greek history, however, it is unsafe to use myth and legend as purveyed in later authors down into the Roman Empire (such as Pausanias) and even Byzantine handbooks; reliance on these flimsy materials produces hypothetical reconstructions which mainly demonstrate the intellectual dexterity and ingenuity of their creators.[10] Contemporary evidence of the eighth century consists only of physical remains from the era; the first step must be to discover what reliable signposts it can provide.

In a provocative, brief communication Snodgrass has recently suggested that two archeologically attested developments of the era are relevant: agricultural changes (by which he seems to mean the expansion of cultivated land and so of population) and the appearance of religious shrines as centers for civic unity.[11] To these should be added the tendency for an aristocratic stratum to appear within the Greek *ethnos* and the outburst of colonization.

Since agriculture was by far the main economic activity in early Greece, alterations here would have important consequences. A change that has been proposed is one from nomadism to true farming, but this had probably taken place earlier in most areas.[12] More likely is a considerable growth of the rural population. This growth is easier to assert than to prove, despite the statistical efforts of Coldstream, Snodgrass, and others. Recently, indeed, a student of the era has argued that the great increase in numbers of graves in eighth-century Attica, usually advanced as a major proof of expansion of its population, may rather attest the evil effects of plague and famine; this seems doubtful, but certainly the rate of growth posited by Snodgrass is demographically unfeasible.[13] Even so the agricultural landscape of Attica and other districts was presumably more heavily settled than in the Dark Ages. Studies of Attic place names suggest an expansion outside the relatively fertile Attic plain proper into the Mesogeia and upland areas.[14] So too the careful exploration of Melos by Renfrew and his aides supports a picture of enlargement of the cultivated area on that island.

Significant political and economic evolution followed. In many districts a surplus of farmers on hardscrabble lands could provide eager candidates for overseas ventures, though colonization was a long protracted process which never at any one point in time matched the large outpouring of Europeans after the shift from sail to steam in the nineteenth century.[15] Against the almost universal misconception that a major lasting factor promoting external expansion was an excess of population, one must keep in mind the demographic principles that a rural landscape tends to remain in balance unless the mode of production changes drastically and that no area can ever truly be overpopulated—if it is, people starve or are weakened enough to fall victim to disease—but that maldistribution of land and power can be influential in encouraging emigration.[16] A well-known model based on African experience has shown that farmers tend to be conservative and to maintain existing institutions, but that if population increases markedly, modes of production will have to be altered to meet the increased needs and so too, by extension, will other aspects of its life.[17] In eighth-century Greece there was surely pressure on contemporary political, social, and also religious organization; an increase in density of settlement gave rise to difficult internal contentions over the ownership of land and the security of personal status.

What may properly be called "government" in an active sense, rather than traditional procedures, became inevitable. Tensions between neighboring communities also emerged as tribal districts were occupied toward their ill-defined frontiers. One need only think, for example, of the contentions over the small Lelantine plain between Chalcis and Eretria, in the years about 700,[18] or the protracted conflict between Corinth and its neighbor Megara, which can be dated to the vicinity of 720 by the temporary successes of the Megarian, Orsippus, Olympic victor at that time (and the first athlete to run nude).[19] By the classical era the boundaries of the *poleis* seem so firmly set that one may forget how much the wars of the eighth and seventh centuries changed the map of Greece, and in doing so required conscious organization of the body politic and military. True political history in a modern sense, however, cannot be constructed from scattered memories even for the seventh and sixth centuries; not until the days of the indefatigable Herodotus does anything like consecutive historical narrative begin to be possible.

The second development noted by Snodgrass in the archeological record, the appearance of shrines as centers of civic unity, may in some ways be accounted as a result of the actual emergence of the *polis*. Clay models and a few ground plans show that the religious buildings of the earlier eighth century were little more than huts, but before the close of the century the first Heraeum on Samos and other shrines were assuming the form of true temples, as the term is defined in archaic and classical Greece. So too reverence of local heroes became evident, as in the cases of Menelaus at Sparta or Agamemnon at Mycenae. Other public buildings could scarcely be expected to have existed at this time—the *agora* as a rule was no more than an open space which could be used for various purposes—but temples were vital signs of political unity.[20]

Scholars who live in a secular age may feel that the erection of temples and the elaboration of public cults were reflections of deeper political alterations, "attendant circumstances" in historical terms; but it is often dangerous to transfer modern attitudes into the past. Even in classical Athens religious business was the first item on the agenda of several meetings of the assembly;[21] religion and state were intimately interwoven, and a mark of citizenship was the right to participate in worship at the shrine of the divine protector: "It is not lawful for a Doric stranger or a slave to be a spectator of the rites of Kore of the Polis," orders a later law of Paros.[22] The functions of the ancient state have been well defined as maintaining the favor of the gods for the community, defending against foreign enemies, and maintaining internal security; in the eighteenth century after Christ the order is different for European states, religion coming last, but the list of duties is the same.[23] In the eighth century B.C. it may actually be that the desire for divine support for the community was a primary, not a secondary, factor in encouraging political unification.

Festivals at the early sanctuaries were a major method of drawing together large numbers of peoples, as the "long-robed Ionians" met to worship Apollo at Delos (*Hymn to Apollo* 147). These centers had economic functions as well. The manufacture of clay figurines always remained an adjunct of shrines, where men and women could dedicate these products to the gods and goddesses who protected their lives and health; before true cities appeared, other types of artisans found their markets in the gatherings at sanctuaries whereas Mycenaean smiths and artists worked for the lords of the palaces. A bronze smithy of the second half of the eighth century has been found in the heart of the shrine of Apollo at Eretria; at that of Athena Itonia at Philia in Boeotia fibulae and even door-hinges were manufactured; at Perachora not only pottery but also ivory and coral were worked, and here a mold for a bronze product turned up.[24] Although the expansion of the use of metals is sometimes overstressed by materially oriented archeologists, the spread of metallurgical skills especially as practiced at the shrines did have its place in promoting the consolidation of society.[25]

The appearance of an incipient aristocracy is a third major element attested in the physical evidence of the eighth century, but one must approach this concept with due caution and discrimination. As Murray has recently observed, "Early Greek society was aristocratic in some broad and general sense, yet we have great difficulty in defining the exact sense in which we use that word 'aristocratic.' "[26] Nonetheless across the late ninth and the eighth centuries richly appointed burials begin to reveal gold earrings, ivory statuettes, and provision of carefully made Geometric vases;[27] an upper class was visibly distinguishing itself from the masses. For a similar development in central Italy also in the eighth century, it has been pointed out that the upper classes may long have been in existence but there became evident only when foreign luxuries were imported and then buried in graves.[28] For Greek lands, however, the equipment of wealthier graves is largely, though not wholly, of local manufacture. It would appear accordingly that the families which commissioned Dipylon amphoras and craters were actually gaining wealth and power. This was surely a potent factor in promoting political alteration, but the word "incipient" has been used deliberately; the appearance of the *polis* must not be construed as a step initiated by the upper classes to gain greater authority for themselves, and so long as the executive authority lay in the hands of a *basileus*—as was usually the case until about 700—a *polis* cannot properly be said to be under aristocratic rule.

Colonization, a fourth development which is apparent from the archeological evidence, has its importance in delimiting a date by which the *polis* had come into existence; the settlement of Greek migrants on many shores of the Mediterranean also widened out the range of Hellenic interests far beyond the confined Aegean basin. Thenceforth, "Greece lies scattered in many regions."[29] These colonies, unlike those of early modern European states, were totally independent political entities, with a few exceptions, which owed only religious duties to their mother state.

Trade led to a resumption of continuous contacts with the far more developed Near East. Some scholars have argued that the *polis* may have been modelled on the tighter organization of Phoenician states, but this is a rather too easy and unlikely solution of the problems under consideration here.[30] Not only is little known of the patterns of government in Tyre or Byblos apart from the presence of kings, but the forces at work in the eighth-century Aegean were principally native in origin. As the latest survey of relations between the Greeks and the Near East comments, Semitic loan words in Greek reflect, above all, trading contacts and not "political, philosophical or even artistic notions."[31]

To summarize the investigation of the physical evidence from the eighth century which seems directly relevant to the appearance of the *polis:* a number of interlocked changes produced problems and advances which would encourage a more conscious political bond among the expanding populations of many Greek areas. Even so, these factors do not seem sufficient to explain the relative suddenness with which the *polis* came on the scene. The Greeks at this time were indeed in a creative ferment, and Hellenic civilization was being set on the lines along which it was to progress in subsequent centuries; sudden jumps were possible in this vigorous environment, but there must have been psychological and spiritual forces, not visible in the physical evidence, which encouraged boldness in political revolution.

Anthropological Models

We can gain useful suggestions for possible answers in a perhaps unexpected fashion by turning to the field of anthropology, which a prominent historian has termed "the most influential of the social sciences" as far as history is concerned.[32] Fortunately for our own search there has recently been a lively debate over the general problem of the origins of civilized states which has produced careful investigation into the typology and stages of development in early societies. At the moment anthropologists are divided between two major, competing theories to account

for the change from tribal organization to the consciously structured state. Both models proceed from the level of chieftainships,
a concept which has already been useful to us in assessing
Homeric society. Yet "a chiefdom is not a class society. Although
a stage beyond primitive equalitarianism, it is not divided into a
ruling stratum in command of the strategic means of production
or political coercion and a disenfranchised underclass."[33]

In the one model economic and social stratification does emerge
and produces a "ranked" society with considerable tension. For
one thing there are "fewer positions of valued status than individuals capable of handling them" (a situation which, as the
conclusion of this chapter will show, was true of some but not all
poleis). Further, there is a shift from communal to private property which is assembled in the hands of a limited upper class,
desirous of maintaining the privileges therewith associated. "The
initial impetus in the emergence of the state is a need to maintain
social order in the face of built-in conflict in a system of differen-
tial access to basic resources," and so in summary "the governing
institutions of the state initially developed as coercive mechanisms to resolve intra-societal conflict arising out of economic
stratification." Thus the state is consciously evolved to defend
the privileges of a dominant class and the sanctity of private
property; primary in the state are systems of public control
(army, police, militia), but the leaders also manipulate modes of
communication to achieve "ideological legitimization of the system of stratification."[34]

Directly opposed to this straightforward scheme is a second
theory advanced by those anthropologists who do not find in
early societies a stratified, propertied class, serious conflict between upper and lower strata, or the use of physical repression.
"These first governments seem clearly to have reenforced their
structure by doing their economic and religious jobs well—by
providing benefits—rather than by using physical force." A strong
central government, in sum, was a gradual evolution as "a response to the need for increased integrative mechanisms in larger
and more complex structures."[35]

At first sight the theory that the state arises as an instrument
of force seems attractive; in anthropological circles it is the most

popular model. It will also appeal to modern Western historians, whether Marxist or not, who have inherited a similar picture of the emergence of modern states out of the medieval world; the employment of military strength is marked in the consolidation of early modern France, England, and other states. So too if one overstresses the power of the incipient aristocracy in eighth-century Greece, the theory appears to gain significant support, and it is of course not solely of anthropological origin. From Hobbes and Locke onward political thinkers have asserted that the state is, in Max Weber's words, "a human community that (successfully) claims the *monopoly of the legitimate use of physical force* within a given territory."[36]

The influence of this point of view, whether consciously or unconsciously held, has been extensive among ancient historians, who often import the concept of class struggle from modern doctrines.[37] Two samples will suffice. Forrest advances a gloomy picture of the ordinary man in 800 B.C. as under the control of nearby powerful landowners "almost as if he were a slave. . . . The many, of whatever level, schooled by centuries of obedience and by the hard facts of life to an unthinking acceptance of whatever rules the *aristos* might impose—this was the *demos,* the people."[38] The sketch is much too black; one may properly ask how motive sources for change could ever have arisen if Forrest's depiction were really true.

Again, in a study based on long thought and deep knowledge, Finley lays down as a fundamental principle that "the state is an arena for conflicting interests, conflicting classes," i.e., politics are a reflection of the struggles of rich and poor, powerful and powerless. Certainly there is always some tinge of such opposition in the history of civilized states, which almost by necessity have upper and lower orders; the marks of conflict can be traced in Greece back at least to Hesiod and perhaps even, as recently argued, in the *Odyssey*. Yet even in Finley's pages the careful reader may find reasons for doubting if this is the basic impetus in forming political structures. He notes, for example, that in antiquity the poor majority accepted the system of government even though the well-to-do did not have at its disposal a large police mechanism; again, there was no argument or doubt about the essential legitimacy of the *polis,* unlike the questioning of the state in the Middle Ages. For this he has "no explanation to offer."[39] Whenever one finds that a thesis fails to cope with systemic problems, then one may suspect that something is amiss in the thesis itself.

The difficulty in the end is the failure of the theory that the state is an agent primarily to repress the multitude to match the actual conditions of the Greek world in the eighth century. The early *polis* did not possess a panoply of institutions of force; families in control of some states such as the Penthelids of Mytilene had a band of club bearers, but they were ineffectual in maintaining the position of their masters; the Penthelids themselves were overthrown without difficulty. Nor is there testimony to destructive conflict of classes until well after the *polis* had become the political vehicle of life; the next chapter will illustrate how the ruthless exploitation by a consolidated aristocracy led to the reforms of Solon and other efforts to assuage economic stress. Kissinger's *Years of Upheaval,* to turn to the modern period, has an interesting portrayal of Japanese statesmen: "The West developed a system of government based on a concept of authority: the right to issue orders that are accepted because they reflect legal or constitutional forms. Japan relies on consensus. A leader's eminence does not imply a right to impose his will on his peers, but the opportunity to elicit their agreement—or at least give the appearance of doing so."[40]

The pattern of political organization and operation which Kissinger finds in Japan seems far more consonant with the eighth-century Greek world than the theory that the state primarily embodies force. In the economic base of the era there was not the great gulf which existed in the Near East; the epics suggest a strong spirit of general communal unity, in which the kings persuade rather than command—a spirit not easily set aside. In the end, thus, the second anthropological model, which, in Service's terms, posits the emergence of the state as a "need for increased integrative mechanisms in larger and more complex structures," surely leads us further in understanding the crystallization of the *polis.*

In exploring the elements involved in these great political

changes I have deliberately failed to draw on the extensive analy-
ses of the *polis* provided by Plato and Aristotle in the fourth century, both because they are far later and because they do not,
except in passing, discuss the origins of the *polis*. Yet one may
note that neither considers the *polis* primarily as a repressive
agent; Aristotle is firm that "a state aims at being, as far as it can
be, a society composed of equals and peers" or again a state seeks
"to secure a system of good laws well obeyed" and has arisen "for
the sake of the general advantage which it brings."[41] Very similar
in tone, and perhaps not accidentally so, is the statement of the
purposes of federal union set out at the beginning of the Constitution of the United States: "in order to form a more perfect
union, establish justice, insure domestic tranquility, and secure
the blessings of liberty to ourselves and posterity." Some modern
historians, following Charles Beard, may be sceptical of these
noble phrases, and it can be argued that Aristotle himself was
blind to the oppression inevitable in slave-holding societies; but
it was he—not we—who did live in the age of the *polis*.[42]

The Early *Polis*

Greek *poleis* are always described as small, in comparison to the
Near Eastern empires or modern national states. Arising early,
when the peoples of Greece lived in self-sufficient enclaves, often
separated by mountains or isolated by the sea, the *poleis* always
thereafter tended to be jealous of their independence.[43] Just
how small, however, the *polis* was on the average has not often
been stressed. Two recent studies agree in identifying 600 to 700
poleis in the course of Greek history, including all the shores of
the Aegean and the islands of the Ionian sea; if one were to add
the far-flung colonies a total of 1500 would not be out of the
question.[44]

The typical *polis*, as a result, ranged between 50 and 100
square kilometers, and its population can be estimated at 625
to 1250 by extrapolation from modern rural densities of the
Aegean islands. If half the citizen body was able to serve as
hoplites—probably an overestimate—then the usual *polis* could
have fielded 225 to 625 warriors. Less than half the states seem

ever to have issued coinage, and then only on special occasions or for specific purposes. The island of Ceos off Attica, only six by ten miles, was divided into four independent *poleis,* three of which coined at one time or another. This range of figures may seem incredible, yet evidence as to the total number of votes recorded in several inscriptions and other evidence is consonant. Finally, one must assume that only about 5% of the population would have held the rural estate necessary to be an aristocrat. Almost none of the *poleis,* as Ruschenbusch points out, suffered from that competition for "positions of valued status" which some anthropologists take as an important element in creating the state; rather, as Aristotle notes, they had to allow reiteration of office or even combination of posts.[45]

Not all *poleis* were of the same scale. There were perhaps 30 middling states such as Megara, Aegina, Sicyon, and others; and at the very top in size and strength were Thebes, Athens, Corinth, Argos, Sparta on the mainland, Miletus, Samos, and Chios in eastern Greece, Syracuse and a few others in the western colonial world. Even these must be placed in proper perspective. Syracuse had a citizen body of some 35,000, Corinth not more than 50,000, and Argos and Thebes would have been of the same order.[46] Only Sparta and Athens were larger; Sparta could field an army of 9000 hoplites, so too Athens during the Persian wars, but the extensive landscape of Attica could not itself have fed more than about 60,000 to 75,000 people. The five states in question were those which were to master the historic stage in later centuries, but even in the eighth century they were exceptional in their expansive powers; as noted earlier, the historic map of Greece proper was established only after considerable change in the eighth and seventh centuries.

If one looks at a physical map of Attica, the area occupied by the *polis* of the Athenians, it is obvious that there are several divisions—the main plain (To Pedion) about Athens itself; the Mesogeia to the east; the communities clustered around Marathon, which always formed a religious union; finally the district of Eleusis to the west. Passes between the mountains range up to 360 meters; Parnes and other heights, over 1000 meters. The Greek term Athenai, a plural form, suggests an initial division, yet this area formed one state of about 1600 square kilometers, whereas neighboring Boeotia, far more open geographically, was always the home of many jarring *poleis*.

One could form a tidy picture of Athenian expansion from a kernel to encompass the eastern and western enclaves, one after another; the end would have been the annexation of Eleusis, which seems to be described as independent under its own *basileus* in the Homeric Hymn to Demeter of the seventh century. This may not be valid testimony in a chronological sense, for the author of the hymn could have retrojected his tale of the wanderings of Demeter; yet at some point Eleusis must have been a separate state.[47] The truth of the matter is that we do not know how and when the Athenians pulled together such a large area; the fact that they did so is a first mark of their political ability, which was to surface again in the times of Solon and then Cleisthenes.

The Athenians themselves, nonetheless, had a detailed legend to explain their union as a deliberate, conscious step by the hero Theseus, who "gathered together all the inhabitants of Attica into one town and made them one *demos* of one *polis*."[48] Earlier there had been differences, even wars, between tribes; but now local council halls and magistracies were supplanted by one common *prytaneion,* a common feast and sacrifice to Athena (the Panathenaic festival), and even coinage with the image of an ox. Thus far Plutarch (*Theseus* 32); Thucydides (2. 15) knew very much the same story in the late fifth century. It is worth observation that Herodotus, always cautious about early myth, refers to Theseus only as exhibiting hubris which displeased the inhabitants of one deme (9. 73). The whole story cannot be given any historical credit, and yet in historical times the Athenians celebrated a festival of the Synoikia. One can only guess that this may have been a creation out of the myth; it cannot serve as decisive testimony in itself, and the picture of a harmonious, united Athenian citizenry scarcely corresponds to the reality of factionalism and local attachments down into the sixth century.[49]

The expansion of Sparta is slightly more visible.[50] When the Dorians invaded the Peloponnesus, they came late in tradition to the valley of the Eurotas river and amalgamated with the previous inhabitants rather than reducing them to subjection;

thence perhaps one may explain the odd fact that the Spartans always had two royal clans and jointly ruling *basileis*. When Sparta became a *polis,* the occupants of the valley itself received full citizenship; those "dwelling about" (*peri-oikoi*) in the hills were citizens without the vote—this incidentally is perhaps the only testimony that from the outset of *polis* life citizens had some political rights. In the eighth and seventh centuries Sparta fully shared in the expanding culture of Greece; at a time when Athens lay in the shade, the choral lyric of Alcman for choruses of Spartan maidens was famous, and Spartans clearly sought luxuries and wealth without reserve. Late in the eighth century, however, Spartan warriors marched around the north end of Mount Taygetus and conquered the Messenian natives of one of the most fertile and well watered areas of the Peloponnesus; since the early Corinthian poet Eumelus wrote a processional for the Messenians at Delos, the conquest must be placed just before 700. This brought immediate riches to the Spartans; it also saddled them with the lasting danger of revolt, the effects of which were to mark later Spartan history.

Athens and Sparta were not alone in enlarging their states or their power over weaker neighbors. In Boeotia Orchomenus and Thebes vied for mastery, and by the end of the eighth century Thebes had gained the superiority.[51] Corinth wrested Perachora and other southern reaches from Megara; Argos destroyed various centers in the Argive plain. Here alone is there archeological corroboration for legend; Asine, which was said to have been destroyed about 720 and its inhabitants driven into flight to Messenia, actually ceased to exist about that date.[52] The expansiveness of the principal states was not to end with the eighth century; Argos temporarily extended its power across the Peloponnesus under Pheidon early in the sixth century and did not eliminate Mycenae until the mid-fifth century, while Athens gained control over Oropos and Eleutherae only during the sixth century.[53]

All the *poleis* of Greece, whatever their size, shared one tongue (though voiced in many dialects), a religious outlook in which the Olympian deities were the patrons of the individual states, and a pattern of culture, which is visible, for example, in pottery styles; already Hesiod and Archilochus use the term "panhellene." Yet toward the close of the eighth century local differentiation of ceramic manufactures is far more noticeable than in the uniformity which had stamped Late Geometric art.[54]

It is often argued that, in the stage of *ethne,* many Greek states had had overarching unity in religious leagues. This may be so, but the Calaurian amphictyony emerged only in the mid-seventh century as a political defense against Argos, and the union of Ionians at the Panionium on the promontory of Mycale also could not have come into existence until about that time, perhaps in reaction to Lydian threats.[55] The most famous union, the Delphic amphictyony, does have an archaic cast as its initial members voted as *ethne* rather than as states, but its first significant appearance in history came in the early sixth century when it was given control of the oracle of Apollo after the destruction of Crisa in the First Sacred War. Thereafter the amphictyony issued orders against destroying any of its *poleis* or cutting them off from water, but otherwise these religious leagues had little effect on Greek politics.[56]

The continuous tendency of Greek history was to stress local attachment on the political level even while admitting Hellenic cultural unity. In a modern study too little noted because it appeared at the outbreak of the Second World War, the French scholar Martin pictured Greek international life as one of discrete units always potentially at odds with each other, an anarchic structure; as Plato succinctly observed, "Every state is in a natural state of war with every other, not indeed proclaimed by heralds, but everlasting."[57] The benefits of tighter political organization were local, not general.

In this chapter the inhabitants of the more advanced economic, political, and social districts have been seen opting for a conscious unification on the political level as marked by the rapid consolidation of religious cults, the choice of military leaders, and the emergence of law and administration by other agents, who, at least in the larger states, rotated in office. Earlier, in defining the *polis,* it was postulated that the new form of political organization was a structure of regular rules and procedures, but

in a preliterate world these rules can only be inferred as residing
in the memory of the elders; and the existence of true offices of
state cannot actually be proven for the eighth century—they simply do appear as soon as there is written evidence. Use of the
word "conscious," however, does not imply that the appearance
of the *polis* was a deliberate decision taken after abstract analysis, but rather that it was a reaction to the increased need for the
strengthening of communal unity.

Only the initial steps were taken in the eighth century. It is
not safe to be specific about their sequence—where evidence is
lacking one must refrain from speculative guesses—but rather an
effort has been made here to place them in an environment in
which change *could* occur. In biology a mutation may appear for
apparently haphazard reasons, but it will not spread far unless
it is somehow "useful." So too one may argue that in eighth-
century Greece one or another *ethnos* decided to create stronger
bonds. The advantages, both internally and externally, were so
evident that the innovation extended into neighboring peoples
with great rapidity; in both cultural and political spheres progress in the decades just before 700 is more properly called "crystallization" than slow evolution.

Across succeeding generations the structure of the *polis* became more systematized on much the same lines everywhere, but
with minor local variations. The *polis* was always a one-celled
structure in contrast to the complexities of vast modern states,
and even in the fifth century, it must be recalled, fringe areas
remained organized in tribal ways; but the later Western world
may well be grateful to the Greeks for creating a pattern of
political organization in which the citizen had rights and duties
under the rule of law.

CHAPTER IV

Patriotism and Divisiveness

After the appearance of the *polis* the next step logically should be its consolidation. Any student familiar with the history of such nation states as France or England will realize that this sequence did not follow automatically; in early modern Europe stable, well accepted procedures of government were hammered out only over the course of centuries. The English parliament in the days of Robert Walpole, for example, was far removed from the occasional meetings of magnates, knights of the shire, and burgesses in the thirteenth century, assembled to give their Plantagenet masters counsel and sometimes money.

The *polis* was a simpler organ, so its evolution took place more rapidly; but the process of development did not proceed smoothly. Throughout the seventh century there was an intensification of unity, but in counterbalance the aristocracies of the Greek states sought their own advantage in ways which almost disrupted society. Solutions to these problems were attained only in the sixth century.

Parallel advances in literature and the arts did not always move in tidy, disciplined fashion. The elegiac and lyric poets show how ruthlessly egotistical and contentious were the men of their age, proud of great deeds and yet fearful of punishment by the gods for their hubris. Still, the *polis* forms the background of life in the surviving fragments of these poets, and the bits and pieces still available to us from their varied works are invaluable guides in many respects. In chronological order the poets may be placed as follows: early in the century Terpander at Sparta, famous for

his musical innovations but without any certainly genuine fragments, Callinus of Ephesus and Archilochus of Paros; then Tyrtaeus of Sparta; Mimnermus, probably of Colophon, and Alcman
of Sparta almost at the end of the century; Alcaeus and Sappho
of Lesbos and Solon of Athens in the years on either side of 600,
though Solon will concern us more fully in the next chapter. All,
it may be observed, are described as citizens of a specific *polis;*
its institutions are sometimes mentioned, and the citizens are
called "pitiless" in their censure of behavior deviating from
proper patterns.[1]

Developments in the arts, equally magnificent, also attest incomplete resolution of problems. Communities were now wealthy
and proud enough to vie in erecting stone temples in the Doric
style; but unification of its several structural elements remained
incomplete. Even if the Orientalizing stage of pottery was everywhere dominant, in its Proto-Attic form it was so much out of
control that the Attic potters could scarcely export their wares to
any other market. Sculptors began seriously to wrestle with the
presentation in stone and metal of life-sized clothed females and
nude standing males; yet it was not until the next century that
artists fully succeeded in going beyond their Dipylon predecessors
in articulating the human form. The man-centered character of
Hellenic civilization became ever more evident, but the other
quality of the Greek outlook, rational analysis, still remained
implicit rather than conscious culturally and politically.[2]

The Demands of War

Throughout the poetry of the seventh century there runs a common theme, the presence of war or its threat as a main concern
of the state in foreign relations. International strife was endemic;
as Bolkestein observed, "There is one trade, the most extensive,
which Greek society ever knew, which was naturally carried on
by the state, i.e., the waging of war."[3] Success in war or in piracy
was at this time the principal source of sudden wealth.[4]

A major change in the organization of Greek armies exerted
pressures toward a tighter framework of political life. Early in
the century a variety of arms and armor already in existence was

assembled to produce the infantry hoplite, with round shield, helmet, breastplate, greaves, and thrusting spear (unlike the javelins of Homeric heroes); and these hoplites were marshalled in a tight infantry mass, the phalanx, several ranks deep. Down to the fourth century this was the formation for battles, which were brutal encounters of similarly equipped citizens warriors.[5]

From Aristotle onward the political effects of the phalanx have been exaggerated, but they were indeed considerable.[6] No longer did the *basileus* have a vital role in battle; once a phalanx had received its exhortation to fight for the safety and glory of the *polis,* a general stood in rank alongside his equals. The phalanx also required the assembly of all able-bodied men who could provide their own equipment rather than a restricted number of nobles who rode to battle on horseback; perhaps as many as one-third of the adult male free population could now be expected to serve in war. Modern scholars, again like Aristotle, tend too easily to speak of a politically active "hoplite class," a hypothetical construct, the weaknesses of which will be discussed later. Most immediately necessary were procedures to make certain that a wider range of citizenry than just the aristocracy should assemble in the phalanx, despite the dangers of battle. Whereas Agamemnon exempted one man from accompanying him to Troy on the payment of a horse (*Iliad* 23. 296–97) in the *Odyssey* (14. 239), it is the *demos* which forces Idomeneus and other Cretans to join the Achaean expedition, and in historical times the openly expressed views of one's "pitiless fellow-citizens" were undoubtedly persuasive to the recalcitrant. In classical Athens informality in this regard had been replaced by a regular writ in law against skulkers and cowards.

On behalf of the community the poets demanded loyalty through positive praise of patriotism. In the first surviving fragment of Callinus, the young are urged on to bravery: "For 'tis an honorable thing and a glorious to fight the foe for land and children and wedded wife." If one dies in battle one will be mourned by all the *laos,* and in life will be a demi-god as a tower for the community. All this, to be sure, could have been said in Hector's day;[7] in the poetry of Callinus' contemporary Archilochus, a soldier of fortune and servant of the god of war, platitude is replaced by brutal frankness about the nature of war as well as zest in battle. While the faint-hearted is disdained, Archilochus engages in conscious, thoughtful analysis of the qualities of a true general, "bandy-legged, feet well planted on the earth, solid of heart" (fr. 93), and can even admit that in rout he threw away his shield and ran—after all he can buy another just as good (fr. 13). True professionals know when to abandon a stricken field; it is the amateur who stays and is slain.

With Tyrtaeus, who wrote a *Politeia* and *Eunomia,* devotion to the *polis* is unmistakably and forcefully urged on the youth. Better is it to die for the fatherland than to leave *polis* and fields and beg, wandering with parents, children, and wife. Tyrtaeus asserts that a man becomes *agathos* or distinguished in war; bravery is the source of *arete,* and defense of the *polis* and all the *demos* is imperative. Tyrtaeus sang his eulogy of patriotism at a critical time in Spartan history, when his fellow countrymen had, at least in tradition, to fight 20 years to put down a stubborn Messenian revolt; the vigor of his poetry may well have been aimed to counter reluctance of Spartan warriors to persist in the struggle.[8]

Consolidation of Government

Not only spiritual unity but also a tightening of political organization were forced on the *poleis* in the seventh century. The most remarkable surviving evidence in this matter is the deliberate recasting of Spartan government. Plutarch in his life of the mythical Lycurgus quotes a constitutional document called the Great Rhetra:

> After you have built a temple to Zeus Syllanius and Athena Syllania and after you have divided the people into phyles and obes, you shall establish a council of 30 elders, the kings included, and shall, from time to time, call to people in apella betwixt Babyca and Cynacion, there propound and put to the vote. The people have the final voice and decision.

In form this is an oracle from Delphi issued in the first decades of the seventh century, but that it is genuine has rightly almost always been accepted; Tyrtaeus, after all, refers clearly to its provisions.[9]

First comes, as is proper, an order to house deities of state, and then an amazing recasting of the people, previously grouped in the usual three Dorian tribes, into territorial wards (*phyles*) and military districts (*obes*); reorganization of tribes and voting districts elsewhere, as at Sicyon, Corinth, and Athens, was not to take place for at least two or three generations. The organs of government were to consist of a council of 30 senior citizens, including the two *basileis* (the elders in subsequent history were elected for life) and an assembly of the *demos*, which had the final right of decision. A later rider, added by the *basileis* Polydorus and Theopompus, laid down the limitation that if the people voted "crookedly," i.e., reached a solution distasteful to the leaders, the assembly could be dismissed as perverting the advice of the council. The formal power of the council to prepare business, "the probouleutic function," is not otherwise attested until the time of Solon at Athens; and the role of the *demos* is for the first time stated clearly. Since Sparta, however, never proceeded further in giving full opportunity for the *demos* to voice its views, it may properly be called an arrested democracy.[10]

In the poetry of the seventh century the *demos* is often mentioned as an element of significance in the *polis*,[11] but the only other occasion on which it appears as an active entity is in the effort of Cylon to establish a tyranny at Athens about 632. His attempt failed, and he and his followers retreated to the Acropolis, where they were besieged. Herodotus and Thucydides disagree as to whether it was the archons or the leaders of the naucraries who assembled the *demos* to conduct the siege, but they attribute an important role to the people. The naucraries, which were evidently in existence at Athens by this time, are obscure in function but may have provided ships on occasion (probably from private ownership); they also had a fund from which treasurers, *colacretae*, could cover the expenses of sacred embassies and the like, though how they did so before the emergence of coinage must remain unclear.[12] Financial structures for the community were thus slowly beginning to appear.

Another major step took place in the field of public rules or laws. As Snodgrass has observed, from early times "there was an established sense of rights of the individual citizen; one of these rights was that of a degree of free communication and, on some issues at least, of criticism."[13] Many modern students look at the seventh century primarily in terms of lawgivers and tyrants; but in emphasizing the former aspect they may sometimes have been misled by another transfer from Roman history, this time the conventional interpretation of the publication of the Twelve Tables as an effort to appease plebeian pressures (which may not in itself be entirely valid). Certainly in Greece there is no testimony that the *demos* was an independent agent in its own right in political processes during the seventh century. At Sparta the *demos* does bulk large in the Great Rhetra, but if tradition is correct this constitutional reform was the product of consultation at Delphi, a step surely carried out by the aristocratic and regal leaders of Sparta. So too at Athens in the later seventh century the reforms of Draco and Solon, though moved at least in the latter case partly by general unrest, were introduced in large part to cope with aristocratic factionalism. Nor, when we come to the tyrants, will it appear that they gained their mastery primarily by popular support.

The transition of law, nonetheless, from oral tradition to written form was a necessary step in the consolidation of the *polis;* though wide-scale reform is unlikely to have been essayed in this process, the power of the state was emphasized, and its rules of government and justice were clarified.[14] Archilochus already knew that Cretan states had laws, and for the last time in Greek history Crete seems to have been a leader for other *poleis;* the earliest surviving law on stone, from Dreros, regulates the tenure of the office of *kosmos,* the major executive officer.[15] Aristotle names two lawgivers, Pheidon at Corinth and Philolaus at Thebes, because of their efforts in a crucial issue, the maintenance of the landholdings of citizens;[16] the famous if almost legendary Zaleucus and Charondas of the early seventh century, active in south Italy, may have tried to harmonize codes for colonies of settlers drawn from many communities.[17]

The Greek alphabet had been adapted from a Phoenician

prototype about the middle of the eighth century, not for economic reasons (Greek contracts long remained oral) or religious utility; rather it arose in a purely secular environment, partly perhaps to set down the Homeric epics. Only in the seventh century, however, do laws, tombstones, and other written materials appear in some volume. Literacy was thereafter to help markedly "in the rise of the kind of critical and rational approach that is prominent in aspects of Greek thought;"[18] politically it was also to be useful in promoting, orderly structured government in which law, rather than the arbitrary whim of a master, directed public life. In the sixth century Phocylides voiced the Greek emphasis on law in a short poem: "The law-abiding *polis,* though small and set on a lofty rock, outranks mad Nineveh," and Alcaeus had spoken of the reunion of a divided host of men "by inspiring it with law and order"; a much later historian was to find the uniqueness of the Greeks in the importance of laws "by which most of all the spirit of the Greeks differs from that of the barbarians."[19]

Finally, though not least in importance in promoting political cohesion, the machinery of religion expanded considerably in the seventh-century *poleis.* Every state with the necessary resources erected a fitting stone temple in which to house the statue of its patron divinity; this temple was located in a *temenos* or sacred, open place—unlike the chapels in Minoan and Mycenaean palaces—which could also be decorated by trophies of victory, statues, and other dedications. Later on, temples were built by means of small contracts under the control of public committees, but the stone itself was provided by the community; whether formal contractors for the detailed work were needed in earlier centuries is uncertain. It is also unclear how the expenses of temple construction were financed, other than by a tithe or booty. Only small crews were required to lay the basic stonework, but timber often had to be imported, and skilled sculptors had to be recompensed for embellishments; Corinth became the center for the manufacture of rooftiles, purchased for many temples in other states. All in all, communal resources had to be committed here more than in any other public activity save warfare.[20]

In the Homeric epics the *basileus* usually appeased the gods and with the aid of seers obtained divine guidance. These functions in the historic *poleis* were in the hands of priests who were, in a modern sense, civil servants rather than religiously dedicated individuals; at times they were publicly appointed, in other cases served by inheritance. The needs of the state cults for sacrificial animals and cult utensils were a continuing, heavy burden on the economic strengths of the *polis*. The first beginnings of public administration seem without doubt to have been the product of the need to safeguard and to inventory temple treasures, to provide technically skilled personnel for cult ceremonies and the determination of divine will in critical issues, and to set down laws for the regulation of such matters.[21]

International festivals and shrines such as those at Delphi, Delos, and Olympia also developed rapidly in the seventh century as centers for athletic competition which provided opportunities for aristocrats to exchange views and information;[22] but these centers were interwoven into the texture of the Greek communities. The oracle of Apollo at Delphi began to offer guidance to the problems of the states, as in the selection of sites for colonies or the issuance of the Great Rhetra; success in the contests brought honor to a *polis,* which rewarded its triumphant citizen ever more munificently—by the sixth century one victor from a south Italian state could build a rural temple with a tithe of these rewards.[23]

The Aristocratic Way of Life

Beside the military, political, and religious moves toward more conscious civic unity and pride there was an impetus driving the Greek world in quite another direction—toward individual self-assertion and disregard of communal demands. The focus was the consolidation of an aristocracy with a distinct way of life, a subject so important that it must be viewed widely in all its social, cultural, and economic implications.[24]

From the period of Archilochus onward the aristocratic ethos which existed in historical times and received its final formulation in the *Nicomachean Ethics* of Aristotle is visible in Greek literature. The famous phrase for nobles came to be *kaloikagathoi,* as distinguished from the *kakoi* or base; but in the seventh century one cannot be sure that its constituent parts, *kalos* (beautiful = polished) and *agathos* (good = preeminent), referred normally to class position rather than to individual merit.[25]

In any event such moral or esthetic standards were a later refinement; more fundamentally, an aristocrat was one who was born into an aristocratic family. As Plutarch once commented, "How often in Simonides, Pindar, Alcaeus, Ibycus, and Stesichorus is 'good birth' *(eugeneia)* a matter of praise and honor?" Already in the *Odyssey,* when Menelaus greeted Telemachus and the son of Nestor, he observed, "No bad stock *(kakoi)* would produce men like you"; one fragment of Archilochus runs, "Enter, because you are well-born *(gennaios)*"; at Athens the members of the upper class were called Eupatrids, men of noble fathers.[26] After the *basileis* disappeared in most states, there were no hereditary titles, though Sappho could celebrate her friend Andromeda as "the daughter of kings";[27] but the leading families of every *polis* maintained an essentially closed circle and displayed a sure sense that their outlook on life was morally superior.

If an aristocratic pattern is to be vigorous, it must be transmitted firmly from generation to generation. Normally the values of the upper classes were absorbed by the young within their families and surrounding groups; but as time progressed formal schools were established.[28] Nobles, thus consciously guided by example and by education into the proper paths in childhood, as adults were subject to constant scrutiny by their peers, at times in communal meals, and by their inferiors in the *agora;* an aristocrat must exemplify the virtues of his class. Public reputation was derived from the judgment of one's fellow men, which was expressed in adjectives such as *agathos* or nouns such as *time* and *kleos,* and success in gaining glory is reflected in the poetry, in the statues in the shrines, and in a variety of other commemorations.

Greek upper classes were as linked on an international plane as were those of early modern Europe. The marriages of tyrants and their children to foreign wives are often mentioned in the sources; but at Athens especially there is evidence for the ties of noble families to many parts of Greece—foreign marriage, though, could always leave the descendants open to the charge of being "of bad parentage."[29] Guest-friendships continued to be as important as they had been in the epics; aristocrats never knew when they might be forced into exile or otherwise need friends in other states. A fragment (13) from Solon significantly describes a happy man as one who has "dear children, whole-hooved steeds, hunting hounds, and a friend in foreign parts."

The aristocratic attitude which was consolidated on the local level and reenforced by foreign ties led eventually to the fourth-century concept of culture (*paideia*). It is, however, dangerous, to transfer the ideas of Isocrates, Plato, and Aristotle back to earlier centuries or to interpret *paideia* as a purely aristocratic outlook. Aristotle's *Nicomachean Ethics* is a forceful expression of contempt for "the utter vulgarity of the herd of men," who live the lives of cows, in contrast to gentlemen who seek virtue; yet in the same work Aristotle takes *communis opinio* seriously and even proclaims, "What all men believe to be so, I say is so; the man who destroys this foundation for our belief is not likely to say anything more convincing."[30] For the Russian gentry of the nineteenth century it has been observed that "their faith, their tastes, their essential fears and hopes were the same (although they little suspected it) as those of the common people, whose ignorance they sneered at."[31] Anthropological studies of peasantries also do not support the view that their culture is essentially different from that of the elite.

Fundamentally the Greek upper classes shared the values of Hellenic civilization as a whole, though they voiced and exemplified those views in a more conscious manner. Yet there were certain aspects in which they did differ. A masculine stamp on society pervaded all ranks, but on the upper-class level male homosexuality came to be accepted as a means by which elders could shape their juniors in aristocratic gymnasia; on the other hand prostitutes thenceforth are noticeable, even famous—and of course had somehow to be paid; Archilochus (fr. 91) asserted that a fortune built over a long period went into the stomach of a *porne*. Aristocratic males continued to assemble by themselves, apart from the commonalty, for purposes of relaxation and political decisions; Archilochus spent much of his time in banquets, and Alcaeus at the end of the century plotted revolt or cursed his Lesbian opponents in *symposia*.

Aristocrats treasured their leisure; no gentleman could work. But one cannot spend one's life entirely idle; men vied in athletic competitions and hunted wild life so ruthlessly that boars and other large animals retreated into the mountains—hunters are depicted on vases with just a brace of rabbits.[32] Above all, the wealthy maintained horses and, if very well-to-do, four-horse chariots, which they could enter in the prestigious races at Olympia; proper names compounded with "hippo-" are common, and horses are the principal animals in figurines and later in sculpture. Since horses were of little agricultural use in the Greek landscape, which was poorly provided with pasture, they are a prime example of what Thorstein Veblen labelled "conspicuous consumption."

Habrosyne or luxury is a leitmotif in the poetry of the seventh and sixth centuries, for aristocrats lived as well as their limited means permitted. They bedecked their women with jewelry and embroidered robes; males too, such as those of Xenophanes' Colophon (fr. 3), "learnt useless luxuries of the Lydians while they were free of hateful despotism, and went into the marketplace clad in all-purple robes, went not less than a thousand in all, proudly rejoicing in gold-adorned hair and bedewing their odor with studied anointings." Much the same picture is drawn by the poet Asius of the Samians (fr. ep. 200): aristocrats are "swathed in beautiful vestments, with snowy tunics that swept the floor of wide earth; and golden headpieces surrounded them, like cicadas; their tresses waved in the breeze and their golden bands and bracelets wrought with carving circled their arms." Thucydides incidentally observes that Athenians gave up wearing golden cicadas in their hair only shortly before his own day.

The expenses of courtesans, delicacies of the table, horses, robes, jewelry and all the other marks which distinguished aristocrats from the *demos* had somehow to be paid. Initially fine linens and other manufactured products came from eastern lands; but by the seventh century they were largely provided by local artisans. The vital question is not the supply but the means by which the upper classes gained the necessary *chremata* or wealth, defined in an era before coinage as "silver and gold and fields of wheatland and horses and mules" (Solon fr. 14).

Aristocratic Search for Wealth

The seventh century actually was marked by a fierce competition for public honor and a raw, undisguised drive for riches scarcely ever again equalled in ancient times, and one which came close to destroying the spiritual unity of the *polis*. Hesiod had already praised the competitive spirit so long as it was just: "Potter is angry with potter, and craftsman with craftsman as he hurries after wealth." In the next chapter a middling range of farmers, the *kakoi* as they were sometimes termed, will come into view as prospering economically by fair means and foul; but aristocrats did not linger behind. Archilochus knew the idea of wages; Alcaeus quoted the aphorism, " 'Wealth makes the man,' and no poor man is noble or held in honor," which he ascribed to the Spartan Aristodemus; his contemporary, Solon, asserted that "those who are richest have twice the eagerness that others have."[33]

But what avenues to wealth were there in a still simple society? Greek warriors served as mercenaries for the kings of Lydia, the pharaohs of Egypt, and the lords of Babylon, but most of our evidence attests their employment at the end of the seventh century or later.[34] So too men such as Solon and Sappho's brother engaged in overseas trade—aristocrats, after all, were those who had the surplus capital and daring for such ventures—but here again their commercial enterprises must be connected with the great surge of trade in the last third of the seventh century.[35] The revenues to support the modest luxury of Greek aristocrats had initially to be derived from the land, first from their own estates but also through an exploitation of neighboring smaller farmers which was facilitated by their control of the machinery of state. In 600 many small farmers had been reduced to the level of peasants, dependent on the greater landowners or even virtually enslaved.

The manner in which loans became so mighty a machine of

oppression is mysterious; but often in history the initial cause of rural distress is entrance into a market system where rewards and losses are outside the farmer's control. When debt does begin to appear in the countryside, as it did also in the burgeoning economic life of Rome in the fourth century, it tends to mount inexorably through the processes of interest and fluctuations in crop yields. What is clear is the end product especially, but not exclusively, at Athens; by the time of Solon "the many had, so to speak, no share in anything."[36]

Aristocrats could now use the *polis* toward their own ends, for they had in most states set aside the *basileis* by the seventh century. *Basileis* continued to exist in far-off Cyprus, always in Sparta, and for awhile yet in Argos, but otherwise they faded away. Precisely how they went we do not know, for historical evidence is sparse.[37] The myth of the abdication of King Codrus at Athens, though dated much earlier in tradition, might suggest a rather sudden end; not all rulers, perhaps, voluntarily placed their heads on the chopping block. A fascinating tale recounts the murder of the *basileus* Cnopus at sea by flatterers who "wanted to destroy his monarchy in order to establish an oligarchy."[38] Aided by their fellow aristocrats of Chios they seized the *polis,* killed partisans of the *basileus,* and then exploited the courts of justice at their own whim so that they could enjoy elegant clothing, elaborate coiffures, and banquets. The story combines nicely the elements of upper-class misrule and the reasons for its rise, but it comes from too late a source to be very trustworthy.

The general lack of legends along this line, nonetheless, cannot be accidental. By and large the *basileis* quietly disappeared as effective leaders of the community in the three functions assigned to them by Aristotle: leadership in war, offer of those sacrifices which did not require a priest, and administration of justice.[39] A fundamental weakness was the fact that the *basileis* lacked extensive economic resources of their own beyond their royal *temenos* or estate, from which they had to provide communal feasts and themselves partake of the life of growing luxury. In a similar situation in early modern Europe the far more powerful kings of the new national states, who could impose taxes

of some types and raid the resources of the Church, had difficulty enough in keeping their exchequers semi-solvent. When
the *poleis* turned to erecting temples or needed to improve guar-
antees of justice, the *basileis* were in too weak a position to become executors of the common will; temples in particular developed their own independent administrations and treasurers. The
final blow probably was the rise of the phalanx form of military
organization which reduced the usefulness of a permanent war
chieftain; what was now needed was a "bandy-legged" general
who could carry out sacrifices to the gods and maintain a discipline which rested mainly on a collective will of patriotic citizens. It is not often noted that Archilochus speaks of a *strategus*
or general, not a *basileus;* and that, perhaps in reaction against
the epic praise of Agamemnon, he describes the qualities of a
general in realistic terms. Such leaders could be changed frequently.

The end result, which alone can be seen, was first the replacement of the hereditary, lifetime chieftain by a public official
(*prytanis, archon,* etc.) who was elected for one year, often at
the outset from a prominent family such as the Bacchiads of Corinth, a fine example and the only one reasonably well known.[40]
Secondly, the other powers once held in a single pair of hands
were parcelled out to a war leader (*polemarchus, strategus*) and
a chief priest (still called *basileus* at Athens so the gods would
not notice the earthly change in the official with whom they were
accustomed to converse). Thirdly, the power of the council
(*boule*) was greatly enlarged as a standing vehicle of aristocratic power.[41] Public buildings now began to be necessary. Sappho mentions a building for officials at Mytilene, where the leaders feasted; the council sometimes met in its own chamber; and
the *agora* became an important center of public activity.[42] The
machinery of government in the *polis* was thereby much strength-
ened; but the critical problem was: How would it be employed?
At Athens and elsewhere the answer was that it would be used
for the narrow, grasping ends of the powerful aristocracy; but in
their demonstration that government could be shaped for personal purposes they had provided a dangerous precedent in respect to their own lasting mastery. Already in Archilochus the

ancestral order can be challenged, for he himself comments on the possibility of securing tyranny for one's gain.[43]

With respect to the speed of advance in Greek civilization, the rule of the aristocrats was of incalculable value. Remarkably open in mind and free from prejudice, they seem scarcely to have boggled at any novelty, whether it was the beginnings of philosophic thought in which events were explained as the product of earthly forces rather than of divine will, or the continuous evolution in the arts. All authors throughout the seventh and sixth centuries, save the ex-slave Aesop, came from an upper-class background; and normally expressed its values in their works. Gentlemen were not likely to subject themselves to the physical labors of sculptors, potters, and smiths, but they directly commissioned most of the artistic production of the age.[44] They thus put an aristocratic stamp on Greek civilization, which through its Roman intermediary continued to mark Western thought down at least to the nineteenth century—subject always to the proviso, already noted, that upper-class values in their basic quality were those of Hellenic society as a whole. It is from the Greek experience that Jaeger could assert, "Culture is simply the aristocratic ideal of a nation, increasingly intellectualized."[45]

But the powerless masses of the late seventh-century *poleis* had no reason to consider this aspect a sufficient counterbalance to their oppression. Divisions between rich and poor and the factionalism of noble families were dangerous threats to the endurance of the *polis*. As Aristotle observed of Crete, nobles could break up the people into clashing groups and produce internal strife (*stasis*). "Such a state of things simply means the disappearance of the state and the dissolution of political society."[46]

Thus far the increasing threats of war and other public needs had helped to produce a partial consolidation of state machinery, the writing down of laws, and the development of religious administration, including the construction of temples in stone. On the other hand, as just noted, the crystallization of the aristocratic way of life sharpened divisive forces. Fortunately a sense of communal unity survived from the incipient stage of the *polis* to support successful efforts at reform.

CHAPTER V

Upheaval and Reform

By the late seventh and the sixth centuries Greek artistic output had soared in volume and variety. The ratio of temples erected in the seventh as against the sixth century is 1:3; for *kouroi* or male statues, 1:5; for *korai* or female statues, 1:4. In these latter examples the ratios must be reduced to some extent to compensate for the fact that stone statues were not carved throughout the seventh century, yet the general order of growth is unmistakable. Even though a count of all the Corinthian and Attic vases would be an impossible task, one may conclude impressionistically that the increase in production here too was tremendous.

Overseas trade began to be really extensive from the later decades of the seventh century onward, and the range of commerce also was enlarged.[1] A trading post at Naucratis in Egypt was founded just before 600; colonization in the Black Sea, primarily sponsored by Miletus, provided new footholds; the Corinthian impetus opened up all the Adriatic. Massilia in southern France was settled about 600 and soon expanded its trading area down the coast of Spain as far as Carthaginian power permitted and inland among the Celtic population of Gaul.

Schumpeter once dryly observed, "Secular improvement that is taken for granted and coupled with individual insecurity that is acutely resented is of course the best recipe for breeding social unrest."[2] If one may dissent from the common view that Greek history is to be cast in terms of class struggle, this reserve does not force one to conclude that social conflict could *never* play a major role. The era 650–550 was deeply agitated as a consequence of the social and economic changes surveyed in the preceding chapter; to recapitulate the result of these changes, the aristocrats had gained mastery over both state and society in the earlier seventh century and often used their power for personal profit. In the larger *poleis,* moreover, contention for the prestige of office tended to rend the body politic.

Examples of the latter problem abound, and several will be considered later in connection with the rise of tyrannies, such as the factions at Athens which facilitated the rise of Pisistratus. At the close of the seventh century an even more vicious struggle afflicted Mytilene, though this did not produce a tyranny. As noted in an earlier page, club bearers had not been able to keep the Penthelid family in control, but its removal opened the door to rancor and public discord. The main evidence for the troubles consists of the poetic fragments of Alcaeus, numerous but not always in adequate context; what is unmistakable is that Alcaeus assailed his opponents Myrsilus and Pittacus without mercy or common decency. Although he professed concern for the "ship of state" in several poems—a metaphor which he apparently coined—this was largely a mask for his own ambitions; his associates were willing to sell the independence of the state to Lydia if aided by its gold. Alcaeus himself was driven abroad, no longer able "to hear the herald summon the assembly and the council";[3] so too Sappho was exiled, though her surviving poetry does not often comment on political affairs—aristocratic anger spared no part of a defeated foe's household, and led at times to massive expulsions of large parts of a citizen body.[4] Scholars have sought vainly to identify economic factors in this unrest, which seems to have been entirely motivated by aristocratic rivalry. The public choice of Pittacus as *aisymnetes,* a role like that played at Athens by Solon, reduced the fever; the much later historian Diodorus asserts that he was successful in ridding the state "of the three worst calamities, tyranny, faction and war" (9. 11).

Conflict of rich and poor, however, did lead to open civil war in several states. After the tyranny of Theagenes at Megara (*ca.* 640–620) an oligarchy assumed power, and in its turn was overthrown by a revolt of debtors who demanded and gained a return of the interest on their debt; matters passed on to the plunder of the houses of the rich, even the murder of pilgrims to Delphi. This went too far, and somehow the Delphic amphictyony rallied forces which put down the uprising and punished the offenders by exile or death.[5] At Miletus there was rural discontent over two generations—at one point the rebellious peasants seized the children of the rich and flung them on the threshing floors, where they were trampled by oxen. Eventually the Parians, called in as arbitrators, settled the government of Miletus into the hands of those who farmed their lands well (i.e., oligarchic elements which were not necessarily of the aristocratic class).[6] Outbreaks of civil war are also known to have taken place at Samos, Syracuse, and other states; as a rule the evidence is too limited to distinguish aristocratic in-fighting from uprisings by the oppressed elements of the countryside.

Although one cannot write a connected political history of the late seventh and sixth centuries, development did not consist solely of civil strife and faction. At Chios, for example, reorganization of public machinery took place which was not necessarily linked to serious contentions, though its tenor is surprising. A poorly preserved inscription, now dated 575–500, speaks in its opening lines of demarchs as well as *basileis* and more clearly ordains that the "council of the *demos*," consisting of 50 men per tribe, is to meet monthly and hear complaints, for which it can assess fines.[7] Here and elsewhere non-aristocratic elements were increasing in strength, an important factor the significance of which will be discussed in the next chapter. Even within aristocratic circles there was at times sufficient opposition to upper-class oppression to permit the choice of Pittacus at Mytilene and Solon at Athens to restore public order.

Cities, Coins, and Thinkers

Although reformers and tyrants in the later seventh and sixth centuries must be placed in a rural context, new institutions and attitudes were exerting great influence on the framework of Greek intellectual and economic life. These included the appearance of true cities, centers in which coinage was the standard for exchange. Further, political and cultural expression of thought became more cohesive.

If one defines cities in terms of temples and public buildings, then they were uncommon down well into the seventh century; alternatively, distinction of urban centers primarily in terms of resident artisans and merchant sectors could lead one to push the origins of some back into the late eighth century. For Greece as a whole, nonetheless, cities became numerous and vigorous on the turn from the seventh to the sixth century. Deliberate arrangement of public spaces and streets did occur in the colonies;[8] in the homeland development was more haphazard, guided at most by religious considerations and the need for a public open space, the *agora*. The usual result is exemplified by "badly planned" Athens, described in the opening lines of this book.[9] Worthy of note also is the fact that the leading classes lived in the urban centers, not in rural villas.[10]

The one city about which anything can be said in detail is Athens; but in commenting on its evolution one runs the inevitable risk in Greek history of taking a very untypical state as a paradigm. Down to about the end of the seventh century Athens consisted of several villages, separated by open spaces in which the dead were buried. By the time of Solon, archon in 594, the focus of Attic political life was becoming a city; the last private houses in the *agora* ceased to exist at that time, and burial had already been discontinued in the area. Only under the tyrant Pisistratus and his sons (546 on) were steps taken formally to regularize and embellish the nascent city, including definition of its major public open space. Whether there had been a temple to Athena on the Acropolis before this time is debatable; certainly Pisistratus built a home for the patron diety of the state. He may, however, have also been a resident of the Acropolis; only later did it shift from a political center to a purely religious precinct.

Somewhat the same picture of urbanization can be detected at Corinth, and to a lesser degree at other cities;[11] yet one must not exaggerate either the size of the cities or their political place.

Urban populations can only be guessed—that of Athens could scarcely have surpassed 10,000—and the centers themselves were not sharply marked off, either topographically by a wall as in medieval times or politically from the countryside.[12] On the other hand their stimulation of life is not to be minimized or distorted, as in the common modern view that they were parasitical centers of consumption, not in themselves productive. This line of thought follows largely theories developed by Max Weber from his study of eastern German towns and is often reenforced, one may suspect, by the dislike of cities from the days of Plato and Aristotle to the intellectual circles of recent generations; as Abraham Cowley put it in *The Garden,* "God the first garden made, and the first city Cain." In early Greece the rapid spread of cities can scarcely be explained as a reflection of their productive and distributive functions in a vibrant economy, supported by the expansion of commercial and industrial elements.[13] Chios has recently been singled out as "a case of deliberate organization of economic resources" in its concentration on wine, metal wares, and other products so that it had to import grain. In actuality no city over about 5000 could have relied for its sustenance on simple exploitation of the scanty surpluses produced by neighboring farmers.[14] Any larger population needed seaborne grain as well, and imports of foodstuffs as a rule had to be paid for by exports, the products of urban craftsmen. The bustling potters of late sixth-century Athens, vying in artistic skill (one inscribed a vase "as never Euphronius") and sometimes designing their work both in shape and in decoration for a specific market, would have blinked their eyes if they had been told that they were part of a parasitical system.[15]

The appearance of cities did not in itself ameliorate conditions in the countryside. Some landless men might find employment in the workshops, but for the most part ancient methods of agricultural techniques did not change enough to release any large amount of surplus labor. Proprietors of potteries and metalworking establishments had rather to turn to the purchase and use of slaves—Chios was called the first slave state, and at Athens too artisan slavery began to be more noticeable. Cities, rather, focussed and sharpened the change which had been under way to bind the rural population to a market economy with its risks as well as potential profits.

When Cyrus the Persian king conquered Lydia, he sent a general to tidy up rule over the Greek cities on the coast of Asia Minor. They urgently appealed to Sparta for aid, and the Spartans duly sent ambassadors to Sardis to warn him not to molest the Greeks. Cyrus incredulously inquired who these presumptuous people might be; on getting a reply said, "I have never yet been afraid of men who have a special meeting place in the center of their city, where they swear this and that and cheat each other." Even though the tale of Herodotus (1. 153) may be apocryphal, it casts a vivid light on a vital difference between Near Eastern empires and Greek *poleis:* only Hellas had stationary markets in which enterprising individuals played economic roles.

Cyrus might well have added a second point, that the measure of value in Greek markets had come to be coinage, for this too was a novel and fruitful step. According to Herodotus the Lydians invented true coinage in contrast to the earlier use of simple masses of metal or grain, that is, the stamping of small pieces of valuable metals "with recognizable designs together with a standardization of the weight."[16] Very soon thereafter the cities of Asia Minor were coining in electrum, and just after 600 Aegina started to issue silver staters with a sea-turtle design. Corinth began to strike with the horse Pegasus on the obverse and Athena on the reverse; its use of the letter *koppa* clearly identified this mint as against earlier anepigraphic issues. By 500 the concept of coinage had spread to the colonies, and hundreds of mints sporadically or more regularly issued their own coins.

This silver coinage was struck on a broad variety of weights, corresponding to the manifold diversity of the *poleis,* and in denominations too large for common use in small purchases in local markets.[17] It was, rather, a tangible, standardized measure of accounting, useful for the increased public activity of the era, for example, in temple construction and the building of warships; by a great variety of market and harbor tolls and taxes, it was then garnered into the public treasuries. The Greeks as a rule did not suffer either taxation on rural income or poll taxes; revolts or complaints over taxation—unlike modern outbreaks—do not mark Greek history.[18] Trade, on the other hand, especially on the international level "is almost always monetized; it is carried on by a class which, though often individually wealthy, is not commonly as influential politically as the landowners . . . and it is physically channeled through a relatively small number of localities, making it relatively easy to mulct." The earliest epigraphic records of state and religious fines mention "staters," which are references to specific weights; before the end of the sixth century such fines were being expressed in terms of true money.[19]

Coinage thus had a considerable role in increasing the regularization of public life, but, as just noted, this useful development did not necessarily produce any shift in the location of political strength. Nor did the cities spawn a true *bourgeoisie* which demanded a public voice. Artisans and traders became more numerous, and sometimes wealthy and proud enough to set up their own dedications of statues, as on the Acropolis at Athens.[20] In various ways the *poleis* did protect and foster economic activity, as in the improvement of harbors, the construction of a slipway by Corinth from the Saronic gulf to the gulf of Corinth to eliminate the dangerous voyage around the southern prongs of the Peloponnesus, the provision of public weights and measures, and the improvement of judicial machinery. Yet, as always in ancient history, rural elements continued to direct the ship of state.

Beside the appearance of cities and spread of coinage a third, less physical phase of Greek progress had political effects. Soon after 600 the first Ionian philosophers commenced to elaborate a picture of the world and of man as governed by natural law rather than by arbitrary ukase of the Olympian deities. A recent effort to show that their aim was really to give political and ethical guidance to the *poleis* goes too far, but most of these thinkers, all aristocrats in origin, did take part in the politics of their day; and the appearance of conscious political activity may have facilitated the general development of rational analysis.[21] Influence may also have gone in the other direction; Solon advanced the concept that just as natural phenomena are the product of natural law so too public problems could be solved by deliberate reorganization of the *polis* to ensure its governance by law. Later, Archytas asserted that "the discovery of calculation ends faction and promotes unanimity by making relations of rich and poor more precise."[22]

The vigorous life of the cities, connected by trade to all the Mediterranean, helped to speed the transmission of such ideas; the explosive onrush of Greek civilization across the sixth century is scarcely explicable otherwise. "Mind *takes* form," observed Lewis Mumford, "in the city; and in turn urban forms condition mind. . . . With language itself, it remains man's greatest work of art"; Simonides put it more tersely, "The *polis* is the teacher of the man."[23]

Reforms: Sparta and Athens

Among the efforts to cope with the social and economic tensions of a rapidly evolving era, the best known are those at Sparta and at Athens. The crises in the two states were very different in origins and character—Greek *poleis* were becoming ever more diverse in superficial structure—but, of the two, Spartan readjustment was more immediately successful; Solon's career produced only partial solutions to the ills of Athens.

The root of Sparta's malaise lay in the Messenian revolt of 640–620. To this point Sparta had not been noted for its military prowess; a Delphic oracle of uncertain date praised the maiden choirs of Sparta, but lauded the warriors of Argos.[24] The difficulty of reducing the Messenians again to subjection is suggested in the almost frantic emphasis on patriotism in Tyrtaeus' poetry, yet more than poems was required to appease and consolidate the Spartan citizenry. At least on the surface the aristocrats yielded their claims to leisure and luxury and merged themselves in the mass of *Homoioi,* the "equal" or perhaps better the "uniform" as full citizens came to be known.[25] Spartan life thenceforth was famous for its simplicity and outward disdain for intellectual pursuits.

To ensure that Sparta could always immediately produce adequate military strength to repress a Messenian outbreak required a massive reconstruction of the life of its citizens to place them under state control. Spartan male babies were officially inspected at birth to determine if they were likely to grow into strong warriors. At the age of seven boys were removed from their homes and were trained in military arts and athletics in troops under their elders; the ancestral structure of warrior brotherhoods was thus consciously ordered. On turning 20 men became adult citizens but continued to dwell together and eat in common messes, the food for which was produced on plots of relatively uniform size farmed by the Messenian helots. After 30 Spartans could live at home but ate one meal a day with their squads, a ready reserve to back up the force of young men who could be assembled on a moment's notice. In this system women enjoyed remarkable freedom to run home and personal estates and were also trained so that they could produce strong children.

Lycurgus, traditionally the author of the restructuring of life, was certainly a myth. Rather, fairly deliberate decisions must have underlain the strengthening of Spartan political and military organization; by the early sixth century the key elements were in place. Perhaps the five annually elected ephors were leaders in the reforms—oddly enough they do not appear at all in the Great Rhetra, though presumably already in existence—but by the sixth century they were powerful enough to check the *basileis*.[26] The first great ephor, Chilon, was in office in 556 and was called one of the Seven Wise Men of Greece; on military expeditions ephors were eventually assigned to advise the chieftains and probably to report back home any irregularities or abuse of royal power.

The intensification of military training was so successful that Spartan leaders across the sixth century attained mastery over all the Peloponnesian states save Argos, which always maintained a minor but annoying independence of Sparta.[27] Yet the Spartans had no desire to increase the area which they directly controlled— it was enough to keep down the Messenians—so the other states were treated as dependent allies. Although Sparta had a first-rate military system, it was not "militaristic" in the sense of desiring to use that machine, as Rome later did, for ever widening power.[28]

The place of Sparta in Greek history and civilization has, indeed, almost always been badly misconceived. In the seventh and early sixth centuries its potters produced Laconian ware, which was exported to Italy, north Africa, and the eastern Aegean, but after about 550 this form of pottery virtually disappears. Modern critics make the simple inference that this was an inevitable concomitant of the militarization of Spartan life; in rebuttal one must remember first that neither at Sparta nor at Athens did full citizens often sink to plying the potter's trade, and secondly that Corinthian pottery yielded its foreign sales at the same time.[29] The fact of the matter is that Attic black-figure ware was swiftly conquering all Mediterranean markets. Another interesting example of anti-Spartan prejudice is the famous crater of Vix, a huge bronze crater made shortly before 500, transported in pieces to central France, reassembled and buried in the tomb of a Celtic princess near the source of the Seine. This has letters on its frieze of marching warriors to help identify where to place the various parts; these are Spartan in form, but often this fact is simply dismissed on the grounds that Sparta could never have been the source for such a masterpiece. Yet it is clear that Spartan bronzework continued to be dedicated at Olympia on down into the fifth century; there is no real reason to doubt Spartan origin for the crater of Vix.[30]

Politically as well Sparta deserves more credit than it usually receives. Its citizens had been wrenched from private life to public responsibilities and activities which they carried on without serious friction; one should note, however, that the usual pictures of brutal repression of the helots are not entirely justified.[31] The Spartans were loath to extend their direct range of control; they were equally not inclined to favor the ambition of tyrants to destroy the internal autonomy of the *poleis* or to permit any one state to gain undue domination abroad. They launched a naval expedition against the pretensions of Samos to Aegean mastery at a time when Athens had no real navy of its own; all Greek states which fell at odds could safely turn to Sparta as an impartial arbitrator, whose decisions were backed by military strength. The reorganization of Spartan life led to its being the balance wheel of international politics; when the might of the

Persian empire was launched at Greece under Xerxes Spartan generals and admirals were voluntarily vested with command by land and sea of the handful of states which resisted the Persians and achieved miraculous successes in the battles of 480–79. Toynbee, in a rhetorical passage, called Spartan life, like that of the Eskimos, "frozen"; the reality was that the Spartan system was always able to produce leaders who commanded the loyalty of their own troops as well as the respect of the Greeks generally.[32] Sparta, in sum, was the linchpin of Greece down to 500, and it was not artistically backward. Unfortunately for their lasting fame the Spartans did not exact tribute from their dependent states, as did the Athenians in the next century, and so a Parthenon never graced the banks of the Eurotas river.

The afflictions of Athens in the late seventh century were of a very different order, stemming from internal difficulties (though Athenian inability to wrest the island of Salamis from Megara also caused discontent). One recent effort to illuminate the murky origins of the troubles assumes that in the later eighth century there was a shift of emphasis from the city of Athens to the countryside, and correspondingly more intensive rural exploitation.[33] The necessary postulate that large-scale commercial and industrial sectors existed so early has serious weaknesses; moreover the city of Athens did not come into being until the days of Solon himself. But certainly Athenian aristocrats, the Eupatrids, were no different from their peers elsewhere in seeking advantage in a rapidly changing agricultural world. The consequence was rural unrest, the fruit of oppression by creditors who reduced many peasants to the status of *hektemoroi,* bound to turn over one-sixth of their produce. Since debts at this time were secured by the person of the borrower, many men were separated from their farms and sold abroad into slavery; those who remained were subject socially and politically to the larger landlords.

If one turns, however, to Solon's own poetry, the only evidence which can lead the historian to speak with confidence, one finds primarily testimony to the dangers of aristocratic factionalism. At one point he comments that "a *polis* is destroyed of great men," and in a long fragment (3) he grieves over the unrighteous minds of the leaders of the *demos* who produce civil strife. Aristocratic divisivenesss, that is, may have had considerable weight in leading the more sober members of the community to feel that reform was necessary. A first effort had been made about 620 by Draco, who brought homicide under public control because it polluted the whole state. The rest of his laws are lost, but apparently a wide range of social customs was already regulated by *demosia grammata,* which are referred to in one of Solon's own prescriptions.[34] In the next generation Solon was elected archon and reconciler in 594 with wide authority to alter all aspects of Athenian life and political organization.[35]

In whatever light one conceives the root of the problem, it is true that Solon's alert mind saw his commission in a wide context. He emphasized the zeal for extortion and the luxurious life of the leaders; and in describing his reforms he put first his liberation of the land, "dark Earth," from its marks of indebtedness (*horoi*) and the ransoming of those sold abroad. Existing rural debts were abolished, and thenceforth enslavement for debt was banned; the previous ties of well-to-do and poorer farmers were thus significantly weakened. Solon sought further to ameliorate the rural situation by encouraging the lucrative pursuit of olive raising and banning the export of grain. For the first time in Greek history a call for "redivision of the land" welled up, but Solon refused to yield to the demand. In various fragments of his poetry he rejected the idea of economic equality and asserted that the gods give each man his due share in life.[36] Solon was far from opposed to the gaining of wealth, though he strongly reproved its unjust acquisition. He also favored the growth of urban elements by encouraging the settlement of foreigners and by ordaining that every son must be taught a craft by his father.[37]

Furthermore Solon devoted ingenious efforts to cope with the ruthless public actions of Athenian aristocrats, though he preferred the conservative approach of changing social and political organization only in limited degree. He established a council of 400 to serve as steering committee for the general assembly; other provisions permitted anyone to sue on behalf of the wronged and to appeal to popular law courts against improper actions of the magistrates. Essentially the aristocracy as political master was now replaced by a timocracy in which the degree of public participation depended not on ancestry but on the basis of wealth, measured in terms of agricultural produce.

Although a great variety of other legislation is reported by Aristotle and other writers, much of it must be dismissed as later fabrication. Solon is thus reported to have ordained that in time of civil stress everyone must take one side or another; yet a law suit of the late fifth century shows that citizens, at least at that time, were under no such compulsion.[38] Weights and measures may well have been revised, in view of the need to measure grain and wine for assignment of a citizen to his proper class, but the statement that he introduced coinage is directly contrary to the numismatic evidence, which shows that Athens did not coin for another generation.[39]

Underlying all Solon's reforms was a deliberate view that the state should be properly organized and governed to produce *eunomia,* a system of good, well-obeyed laws. As noted earlier, he argued that snow, hail, and thunder were natural phenomena; so too evil events in the state were the product of ignorance by the common citizen, and thus justice was no longer a blessing bestowed only by the gods, as in Hesiod's *Works and Days.* The well-to-do might be the leaders in securing *eunomia,* but all citizens had their responsibilities: "The common evil comes into every house, and the street door will no longer keep it out; it leaps the high hedge and surely finds one, for all he may go hide himself in his chamber" (fr. 3). Thenceforth the *demos* had to be accounted a conscious element in political processes, though Solon himself feared deeply that its participation might be unwise; he had to fight efforts to make him a tyrant and repeatedly stressed his own position as standing between rich and poor, securing each its due but no more than that.

In later days Solon became the most revered figure in Athenian history, a place which he fully deserves for the breadth of his vision and skillful efforts to implement his reforms. As a sensitive recent study sums up his work, "He had taken a traditional society and made it in social terms one of the most advanced in Greece. His reforms might look less radical than those of two generations earlier at Sparta. But whereas Spartan institutions were directed at the hoplite virtues of discipline and courage and the closed society, Athens was set on a more flexible course toward social justice."[40] Yet although his measure did cope with the unrest of the countryside, he was less successful on the political level than were the anonymous leaders who restructured Sparta. Within a decade Athenian aristocrats were again wrangling over tenure of the archonship and power in the state; the eventual result was the tyranny of Pisistratus, which was favored by some elements in the villages and the city of Athens even if his opponents officially raised a full citizen levy against him.

Tyrants

Much ink has been spilled in recent generations over the tyrants of early Greece.[41] All too often, however, the changes of the seventh century are presented in the simplistic, even misleading terms of a popular search for relief from oppression first by demanding codes of laws and then, when these were inadequate safeguards, by seeking the support of tyrants.

Modern explanations of the appearance of tyrants which seek to be more specific have undergone marked shifts as a reflection of the alterations in general views of the causes of historical change. A famous English treatment of the 1920s, which ascribed the appearance of tyrants to economic distortions caused by the use of money and the effort of commercial and industrial classes to break the power of the upper classes, has now been universally rejected. There was, to repeat, no *bourgeoisie* in ancient Greece; and chronological evidence proves that coinage came later than did the early tyrants. A more recent attempt points out that tyrants followed very soon after Greek military organization shifted to the hoplite phalanx; Aristotle comments on the enlargement of constitutions once the hoplite had become important, a view for which he provides no major historical testimony. Even so it is argued that "a sort of middle class, including the more substantial of the small farmers," claimed a voice in public affairs and rallied behind tyrants, if necessary, toward that end.[42]

This interpretation has merit in connecting the rise of tyrants with rural alterations, but it too falls in the end. There was no "hoplite class" as a conscious, unified economic grouping—by what means could such men have reached a sense of solidarity in the *polis?*—and in social terms anyone who could do so aped the ways of life enjoyed by men of inherited wealth and position. Politically as well there is no evidence that a hoplite class in any *polis* actually did facilitate the rise of a tyrant.

During the last few years there has been an effort, among both Marxist and liberal historians, to establish a tie between the social and economic tensions of the seventh century and the appearance of tyrants.[43] Unfortunately the evidence nowhere unmistakeably attests a firm connection. When Cylon tried to seize mastery at Athens, the *demos* as a whole was rallied to besiege the conspirators; Herodotus gives a full account of the situation in which Pisistratus gained power at Athens and presents the causes in terms of aristocratic divisiveness. The more scanty testimony in other states points in the same direction; a coup d'état, after all, is most easily attained when only a small fraction of the population is politically active.[44]

One must not exaggerate the numbers of tyrants as if all the *poleis* were thus afflicted. Apart from the Persian-supported tyrants of Asia Minor only 27 states are known over 150 years to have experienced a tyranny.[45] None existed among the host of tiny states; most appeared in states of the middle range: Theagenes of Megara (*ca.* 640–620), perhaps Orthagoras and certainly his son Cleisthenes of Sicyon (*ca.* 595–575), Antileon at Chalcis and Diagoras at Eretria at uncertain times. On the eastern coast of the Aegean there were Polycrates of Samos (*ca.* 540–522) and Thrasybulus of Miletus (about 600). In the west several Sicilian states had tyrants of magnificent luxury toward the end of the sixth century; earlier Phalaris at Acragas (*ca.* 570–555) had become infamous for having a bronze bull constructed in which he could roast alive his opponents and their moans would appear as the lowing of the bull—not all tyrants were pleasant, urbane patrons of civilization. Among the five great states of the Greek mainland only Corinth, with its Cypselid dynasty (657–585) and Athens with Pisistratus and his sons (546–510) fell under tyrannical rule;[46] these two were also distinguished by the fact that they certainly had a "dynasty" of tyrants, that of the Orthagorids at Sicyon being questionable.[47] As a rule tyranny was too opposed to Greek political values to last more than one generation, if that long.

When one looks at this list geographically and economically, interesting aspects surface. A considerable number of the states lay on the main trade route through the Saronic gulf and gulf of Corinth; all were relatively advanced in commercial and economic pursuits. This fact does not in itself support the concept of an independent *bourgeoisie;* in these states the aristocracies had more incentive to desire luxuries and so to oppress their inferiors more mercilessly, while at the same time inherited ties and groupings were weakening enough here to open the way for able individuals to seize routes to power.

Essentially three intertwined factors produced tyrannies. One was an aristocracy which was divided or had besmirched the fair name of the state by failure in foreign ventures; the Bacchiads abused their control so far that Cypselus was ordered by a Delphic oracle to "set right" the state.[48] At Athens there was continued public anger over the possession of the offshore island of Salamis by Megara until Pisistratus gained it permanently for Athens and then utilized his popularity to elevate himself above the aristocratic factions. Secondly, nobles of ability (especially military) who were self-seeking had to be present to seize the opportunities. And finally almost all tyrants-to-be had to gather a force of mercenaries to help them gain and hold their illegal position. In his final bid for mastery Pisistratus was aided by Thebes, Argos, Naxos, as well as other areas, and paid his troops from the gold of his Thracian mines.[49]

Aristotle baldly but correctly sums up the role of tyrants: "the aim of a tyrant is his own pleasure," and describes the means by which he could break the spirit of the citizens, banning clubs and common meals, the use of secret police, and even the impoverishment of his subjects.[50] Ostentation in daily life and elaborate grave decoration were restricted by the Cypselids and, at least in theory, by Pisistratus; only the tyrants themselves might have a court and often posed as supports of arts and letters. The Pisitratids thus gathered some of the famous poets of the later sixth century, including Simonides and Anacreon (the latter brought to Athens by a state galley) to enhance their prestige,[51] and engaged in a major building program. Pisistratus himself regularized the *agora* and provided a sure supply of water to the city by means of an aqueduct; so too the Cypselids, Theagenes, and Polycrates built fountain houses for their cities—the tunnel through which Polycrates conducted water to Samos was one of the most ambitious engineering feats of the sixth century.[52] The Cypselids fortified their urban center, created a new harbor at Lechaeum, built a slipway across the isthmus of Corinth, and engaged in a considerable amount of temple construction; Aristotle records that Periander relied only on taxes on the *agora* and harbors of the thriving Corinthian trade.[53]

Regular coinage was also issued by the mints of the tyrants, but with motifs as a rule which emphasized the state rather than the individual master; at Athens tetradrachms with the head of helmeted Athena on the obverse and her owl with the letters AΘE on the reverse set the model for Athenian coins for half a millennium. There is, however, no evidence that tyrants directly supported potters and sculptors save by purchase of their products.[54]

Yet the burgeoning urban population was suspect to tyrants; the description of Cypselus as an "able merchant-prince" is misleading.[55] If the tyrants favored any segment it was the middling and smaller farmers, though there is no certain evidence that they redistributed the lands of exiled aristocrats.[56] Pisistratus encouraged rural elements by loans, by improving the roads, and by instituting a system of traveling judges so that peasants would not have to come to the city for justice; on the other hand he exacted a tax of 5% or 10% on agricultural production. At Corinth Periander went further by limiting urban inhabitation; Cleisthenes ordained that farmers of Sicyon had to wear their rural goatskins if they came to town.[57] The economic changes of the seventh and sixth centuries, naturally, could not be halted by such measures, and the cities continued to grow in size; but at least at Athens the resident aliens (metics) were denied citizenship, though numbers did manage to place themselves on the citizen rolls.

Abroad tyrants sought to gain security by marriage links and otherwise pursued cautious policies of expansion which would not bring about a war with another *polis* or with dangerous barbarians; often they had disarmed their citizenry, as Pisistratus did at Athens, and could not place themselves at risk.[58] The Cypselids expanded a network of colonies up the Adriatic, and Periander even had a warlike reputation; Cleisthenes participated in the First Sacred War, designed to liberate the shrine of Delphi from the neighboring state of Crisa; Pisistratus took Sigeum on the Asiatic side of the strait of Chersonesus, and encouraged an ambitious Athenian of noble family, Miltiades, to set up his own principality on the opposite European shore.

Far safer was deliberate elaboration of state cults and ceremonies. Cleisthenes transferred the performance of choruses at Sicyon from the ancestral hero Adrastus to the god Dionysus;[59] for Athens, in this respect, the evidence is especially wide. The cult of Dionysus was brought under state control, and a competition for the performance of tragedies in his honor began in 535 or 533, when Thespis won first prize. Homer also received his due through public support for the recitation of his epics, an event which helped to produce standard texts of the poems. Pisistratus further increased the majesty as well as public direction of the mysteries at Eleusis by building a new Telesterion, oversaw the worship of Artemis at Brauron, and purified the sacred island of Delos by removing the old graves in the vicinity of its temple of Apollo. The annual procession in honor of Athena was enhanced every five years to become the Greater Panathenaea, a festival which remained an important part of the Athenian calendar for centuries.

For Pisistratus it is specifically recorded that he kept the constitution in full force and even appeared in court to meet a charge.[60] A surviving fragment of the Attic archon lists shows the appointment or election of aristocrats. Yet other noble leaders were driven into exile, and in the reign of his sons a wealthy man dangerous by reason of his popularity in winning the chariot race at Olympia three times in a row, Cimon the father of Miltiades, was assassinated by night. Elsewhere there was some change in public organization; Cleisthenes recast the tribes of

Sicyon and so too apparently did the Cypselids at Corinth. Everywhere, however, the element most carefully watched by the tyrants was their fellow aristocrats, for these were the men who might lead the masses in opposition to illegal exercise of tyrannical power or on their own could form private cabals such as that which killed Hipparchus at Athens in 514.

The effects of tyranny in the political evolution of Greece have been very diversely assessed. Helmut Berve, who has written the most thorough study of tyranny, considers their appearance as one of individualistic opportunism and bluntly asserts that they were totally outside the constitution of their states.[61] The opposite point of view is put by How and Wells in their commentary on Herodotus: tyranny "was a necessary stage in the progress of the state"; even though Herodotus had a hostile view toward tyrants.[62] Not all of these masters were as diabolical as Phalaris; Cypselus could walk the streets of his city without a bodyguard, and the rule of Pisistratus was fondly remembered, according to Aristotle, as a golden age of Cronus. Yet on the extinction of the Cypselid dynasty "the *demos* tore down the house of the tyrants and made public their property; they threw [Psammetichus'] body out of the country without burial, dug up the graves of his ancestors, and cast out their bones." Laws against illegal usurpation of power are known at Teos, Athens, and elsewhere.[63]

Insofar as tyrants did gain any general acceptance, there were historical reasons to justify their sole mastery. The epics preserved memory that *basileis* had once been dominant; in colonization the *oikistes* or leader had necessarily been a forceful man, who often was virtually worshipped in the later history of a colony.[64] As Heraclitus observed, "To obey the will of one man is also law."[65] Yet in the changing character of political values it was *not* law: "the aim of a tyrant is his own pleasure."

In the end one may judge that by concentrating power in the hands of one person, tyranny did to some extent increase consciousness of the unity of the *polis,* and public finance in the prosperous states was markedly increased in the form of taxation, tolls, or plain confiscation to meet the expenses for building, bodyguards, support of arts, and other outlays.[66] By their protracted tenure tyrants also weakened the hereditary position of aristocrats as unquestioned leaders of the state. In modern history, as a parallel, the upper classes secured the restoration of kingship in the person of Charles II in England or Louis XVIII in France after civil war or other disruption, but they could not put back the clock to the preceding stage of aristo-cratic domination. By the later decades of the sixth century Greek aristocrats had had to yield control of the political ma-chinery or at least to share it with other groups.

Many of the factors involved in this shift had emerged across the later seventh and early sixth century, including the rise of overseas trade on a much larger scale, the appearance of urban centers in the markets of which coinage served as a standard for exchange, and the sharpening of intellectual analysis. Vicious contentions had bubbled up in many states, but had generally been compromised, though on very different lines, as the reforms in Sparta and Athens illustrate. The states which did not experi-ence tyranny seem to have progressed as much as those which did; the processes of change were widespread and irresistible.

CHAPTER VI

The *Polis* World in 500 B.C.

By the close of the sixth century the *polis* had reached the form which it retained throughout ancient times. Physically its equipment of public buildings was elaborate; the Greek geographer Pausanias had what amounted to a checklist—acropolis, walls, *agora,* temples, theater, gymnasium—which he could expect even the smallest *polis* to possess.[1] Its basic organs of government were also generally uniform: magistrates with well-defined duties elected for one year; a council, normally of elder citizens; and an assembly, usually of all the citizens.

Political power everywhere remained in the hands of men who owned rural lands. Industrial and commercial elements were not totally ignored in the determination of public policies, but nowhere did they form cohesive groups which had any chance to dominate the government. In most states they were a small part of the population, and even in Athens, the largest industrial center, non-agricultural pursuits were often in the hands of resident aliens, though not always.

The ideal for a *polis* was autonomy, that is, the right to establish its own laws and to administer justice without outside interference.[2] Not all Greeks, however, either lived in *poleis* or had this right. Many of the backward areas in the northern and western reaches of the mainland continued to be occupied by tribes. Among the *poleis* proper smaller communities were sometimes dependent on more powerful neighbors,[3] and a number of states were grouped in leagues. The Boeotian league, centered on Thebes, used the same symbol on its coins, a shield, but each state marked its own issues with a letter denoting the specific origin; the league, in sum, was to a large degree a federal union with a supervising board of Boeotarchs in which Thebes only occasionally had a decisive voice. Spartan allies were formally organized late in the sixth century by the vigorous *basileus* Cleomenes; in this Peloponnesian league, as it is named by modern scholars, a conference of representatives from the dependent states met each year at Sparta and usually endorsed its suggestions. Yet on occasion the conference could disagree, as in a refusal to support a second Spartan intervention in Athens in 508; during the tense period prior to the outbreak of the Peloponnesian war in 431 the allies, not Sparta, pressed most vigorously for a declaration of war against Athenian imperialism.[4]

In a larger sense the Greek political system as a whole was about to find itself more continuously influenced by external powers. Down into the sixth century the Aegean communities had developed without serious interference from Assyrian and other Near Eastern empires. Phrygian, Lydian, and Egyptian rulers had found it advisable to maintain friendly relations with this vibrant, expanding society, largely by making dedications at Greek religious shrines; the motive perhaps was to secure valuable mercenaries more easily. In turn Greek aristocrats had at times named their sons after these monarchs, though the reasons for this honor are obscure; the last Cypselid tyrant was Psammetichus, and a tombstone survives of a young Athenian named Croesus, who had died in battle probably in connection with the rise of Pisistratus.[5]

From Alyattes on the Lydian kings had mastered some of the states on their seaboard, and Cyrus consolidated this rule more firmly. A number of the Greeks of Asia Minor reacted to this loss of independence by migrating individually or as whole communities to Italy; those who remained seem to have thrived under Persian mastery. In an abortive effort to conquer south Russia Darius incidentally extended Persian rule over the *poleis* on the north shore of the Aegean. Persia thus became much more involved with Greece; when the Athenian reformer Cleisthenes felt himself endangered by the Spartans he engineered an appeal to the Persian satrap at Sardis, but by the time the Athenian ambassadors returned the situation had become more secure and the danger of Persian interference could be set aside. Soon after 500 several Persian expeditions were launched against Hellas, but all failed. The Athenian counter-offensive in the mid-fifth century kept the Persians off balance until the outbreak of the Peloponnesian war which opened the way for more decisive intervention in Greek politics. All that lay in the future; when the Greek doctor Democedes of Croton escaped from a Persian reconnaissance of the Aegean and made his way back to his native state shortly before 500, some of his fellow-citizens were in fear of Persia but in the end they refused to give him up.[6]

Where the *poleis* varied most markedly at that point was in their practical definition of "citizen," that is, which parts of the population really held political power. Nowhere, naturally, did women, slaves, or resident aliens have a vote; but even if all males could attend the assembly there was a wide differentiation in the actual locus of authority. As a result of the upheavals and reforms of the later seventh and the sixth centuries the aristocracies generally were no longer in sole mastery, but had been forced to admit other sectors to the governing circles. How far this widening proceeded could vary tremendously.

Athenian Democracy

Athens had been unusual in its unification of a remarkably large area and in the wisdom of its leading elements, who chose Solon as archon and reconciler of its political and economic problems. Just before the close of the sixth century its form of government was deliberately recast to make Athens a democracy, again an unusual, almost unique step, carried out primarily by Cleisthenes. His reform may have been impelled by the necessities of practical politics rather than by the idealism pervading the work of Solon, but historically Cleisthenes was far more successful. Athens continued for at least the next two centuries to be the leading example of democracy in the Greek world, and only minor changes were made in its political procedures.

Cleisthenes owed his opportunity to a tangled web of events, which is fairly well illuminated by Herodotus and by the Aristotelian *Constitution of the Athenians*. In 514 an aristocratic cabal sought to kill the sons of Pisistratus, but though the "tyrant slayers" Harmodius and Aristogeiton were later celebrated in verse and by statues in the *agora,* they bungled their attempt and despatched only Hipparchus. His brother Hippias thereafter ruled Athens in a far more vengeful fashion, which alienated most of the elements who had supported his father. One noble family, the Alcmeonids, had gone into voluntary exile, and by contracting to rebuild the temple of Apollo at Delphi after a fire, gained the support of the Delphic oracle, which urged the Spartans to abolish the hateful tyranny at Athens. Since Spartan policy from the time of Chilon had been opposed to tyranny and had engineered its end at Sicyon and elsewhere, the *basileus* Cleomenes was more than willing to hearken to the voice of Apollo and in 510 led an expedition to Athens. Hippias fled to the Acropolis, but when his children were captured agreed to lay down his power in return for safe departure.

Once again the Athenians could engage in factional politics. The conservative leader Isagoras was elected archon in 508 and sought to undo all the changes in the tyrannical period, especially by purging the citizen rolls of aliens who had crept into full acceptance.[7] His opponent, Cleisthenes of the Alcmeonid family, was weaker in electoral support; by way of counterbalance he "called to his aid the common people" with the battle cry of *isonomia* or equal rights.[8] Isagoras appealed to Cleomenes, who came to his rescue with so small a force that in turn he had to retreat to the Acropolis and to evacuate Attica. When Cleomenes sought to muster the full strength of the Peloponnesian league he was rebuffed, as observed earlier, by Corinth and the other allies. Cleisthenes, though still a private citizen rather than archon, was then able to introduce in the assembly a mass of laws which reorganized Athenian government.[9]

The basic alteration was in the recasting of voting districts.[10] Thenceforth Attica was geographically divided into ten tribes; each tribe in turn consisted of three districts: one in and about the city, the other two in rural areas which might be contiguous but usually were separated by some distance. Each of these districts or *trittyes* in turn was composed of one or more demes, normally the pre-existing villages of the Attic countryside. Earlier the basis for claiming citizenship had been acceptance of a son by his father's *phratry;* from Cleisthenes on registration on the roll of a specific deme was the necessary step, though new citizens also did gain assignment as well to a *phratry* by their decree of enfranchisement.[11]

Each tribe provided 50 members for the new council of 500, drawn by lot from candidates nominated by the demes though there is no information on the vital point as to how these candidates were chosen.[12] To safeguard against the danger that the council could become hidden master, like the Signoria in medieval Venice, councillors could not serve two years in a row or more than twice in their lifetime; the council was to be a steering body which prepared business for the assembly and supervised the execution of popular decrees by a host of boards of magistrates, usually consisting of ten members with very specific and restricted functions. Eventually all these boards, save that of the ten generals, were also chosen by lot, and any group expending public funds was rigorously audited; it was easier to get into public offices than to lay down their responsibilities. The Athenians deeply cherished democracy, once established, but had little faith in the incorruptibility of individual citizens. The council was the "regulator," the assembly the "dynamo," which had final and unquestionable authority, though the right of free speech by any citizen who could command the attention of his fellows, *isegoria,* seems only to have established in the early fifth century.[13]

Cleisthenes' reforms show a clear geographical and political knowledge of Attica and were evidently meditated with some deliberation;[14] not all the changes could have been carried out in a few weeks or months. His boldness, to be sure, was not unprecedented. Reorganization of voting districts had earlier been carried through at Sicyon, Corinth, Miletus, and elsewhere; at Corinth the eight tribes were even divided into "thirds" of noncontiguous territory.[15] The Greeks had by now cast off inherited shackles of tradition not only philosophically but in many other reaches of life.

The true aims of Cleisthenes remain the subject of debate, for there is no evidence to illuminate his fundamental attitudes as is provided in the poetry of Solon. Some scholars would emphasize his placement of a wide range of government in the hands of the demes, which could practice democracy on the local level and accustom demesmen to take up their duties in the general assembly. Unfortunately for this argument a variety of later deme ordinances and reports of deme meetings preserved in the Attic orators and inscriptions demonstrate that the landlords of any one area fairly effectively controlled its activities.[16] Others, again, stress the ingenious system of choosing the council of 500 as ensuring that all parts of Attic society had to participate in public life and that the power of earlier local factions was shattered by the redivision of territories;[17] it has been estimated that about one-third of the adult citizenry would at one time or another serve on the council, so that knowledge of the actual processes of government would be shared by the citizen body. Skeptical historians are inclined to suspect that Cleisthenes, in his grouping of demes into *trittyes,* was seeking personal advantage, though it is difficult in looking at the new map of Attica to detect deliberate gerrymander on a wide scale.[18]

In the end the safest conclusion is that Cleisthenes sought to gain popular support in the assembly, and that the mass of Athenian citizens had progressed so far in political consciousness that it was now able to exercise responsibilities; immediately after the reforms Athens met and repelled an invasion by Chalcis and the Boeotians. As Herodotus comments on this victory, it proved "how noble a thing freedom is, not in one respect only, but in all; for while they were oppressed under a despotic government, they had no better success in war than any of their neighbours, yet, once the yoke was flung off, they proved the finest fighters in the world" (5. 78).

Although the leaders of the Athenian democracy thereafter were almost always to be aristocrats, they held power only so long as the citizenry supported them; and by the device of ostracism such great men as Themistocles and Cimon were to be chastised. Overall most citizens remained rurally rooted; yet one must not forget that the assembly met in the city itself and that a considerable part of the urban population was connected with the prosperous trade and industry of Athens, not all of which by any means was in the hands of slaves and resident aliens. The active participation of the citizen body reflected both rural and urban sense of sturdy independence, and though the Athenian democracy made many wrong decisions in the fifth and fourth centuries it basically governed itself well.

Ironically enough Cleisthenes was almost forgotten and never became a figure of reverence; Solon's ideal conception of the state helped to make him a George Washington whereas perhaps Cleisthenes' reforms smacked too much of opportunism—"he did not create the democracy but made it possible."[19] Yet more than once in history opportunists have had greater effects than they planned in seeking their own advantage.

Greek Oligarchies

Athens, it cannot be said too often, was only one of a great mass of *poleis.* Modern books with the title of "Greek Democracy" or the like are seriously misleading, for almost all states by 500 were oligarchic in structure and remained so. Very few were still aristocratic in the full sense of that term.

To explain the shift from the rule of the well-born to that of the well-to-do must lead one far back across Greek history. The indomitable figure of Hesiod first attests the existence of elements which were not aristocratic yet strong enough to demand a place in the conduct of public affairs in the long run. Hesiod is often called a peasant, but he totally fails to fit the modern anthropological definition of a peasant as a rural producer dependent on a secondary group which uses the surpluses extorted from the peasant class for itself and other non-farming groups. Hesiod did not belong to the top level of his society, but economically he occupied an independent position and addressed the bulk of his poem to farmers capable of finding capital for the purchase of a team of oxen and female and male slaves or for maritime trips to dispose of surpluses on their own account. For himself Hesiod sought, in the heat of summer, "a shady rock and wine of Biblis"—imported from Phoenicia at a time when foreign items of any sort were rare and expensive. The practice of farming, in Hesiod's view, might not be successful, but "it is idleness which is a disgrace." On the whole, earnest toil and dedication would bring their rewards, a well-filled barn and rural security. His auditors were, in turn, not aristocrats but men of some standing; they must be kept clearly in mind in looking at historical changes across the seventh and sixth centuries.

In this era smaller farmers did often sink to the level of peasants or, in Thessaly, Messenia, and Crete, to a status which may loosely be called serfdom or, as it is expressed in an ancient term, "between free and slave"; that is, they were farmers tied to their land and owing regular dues to their lords. To some degree their subjection was the unfortunate fruit of market economies, but also it derived from the consolidation of the *polis* under aristocratic control. "It is only when a cultivator is integrated into a society with a state—that is, when the cultivator becomes subject to the demands and sanction of power-holders outside his social stratum—that we can appropriately speak of peasantry."[20]

Others profited from the opportunities opened by the appearance of urban markets and flourished economically. These were men who may be called semiaristocrats, seeking to live in an aristocratic mode, adopting upper-class values, but not able to gain acceptance as peers by the masters of the seventh-century *poleis*. In modern English terms they might be called the gentry;[21] in the poetry of the sixth century they have become more evident and are often described as the *kakoi*, the "bad" as against the *aristoi*. Their greater prominence by this time may simply be the result of a larger volume of information, but it is also probable that in the rapid increase of economic enterprise during the period they found greater opportunities to sell their produce in the markets of the cities and to exploit their weaker neighbors. In the middle of the century Phocylides is earnest in warning "Be not the debtor of a *kakos,* or he will annoy you by asking to be paid before his time" (fr. 6).

The most illuminating discussion of *kakoi* is to be found in the poetry of the sour misanthrope Theognis of Megara, who endured life about 550.[22] Thus far his voice has not appeared in these pages, though alone among early poets his entire work has survived in the *Theognidea,* which also incorporates a great deal of additions on across the fifth century; this didactic material is of great value in showing the environment in which aristocracy yielded to oligarchy. The genuine poems of Theognis himself were largely addressed to his young boyfriend Cyrnus and had the intention of handing on "the counsels I learned from good men (*agathoi*) in my own childhood. . . . This then I would have thee to know, nor to consort with the *kakoi* but ever to cleave unto the *agathoi,* and at their tables to eat and drink, and with them to sit, and them to please, for their power is great" (19–38).

These views were no different from those of Sappho, Alcaeus and other earlier poets, but at this point Theognis had to face a very uncomfortable fact, that in reality the *aristoi* were no longer necessarily the wealthiest members of society, even though poverty is one of man's worst curses. The implications of this change, which appears to have been a recent one, run through all the rest of his poetry. The *kakoi* have often gained wealth, and set no end to their search for gain; there is not one boatload of those who put good ahead of money. The result socially is deceit, wiles, lack of trust and gratitude. Since the *kakoi* are at one point described as having once worn goatskins (54–55) they are clearly of rural origins, but they have waxed powerful in the city. In Theognis the term *demos* first begins to have a pejorative meaning as socially inferior.[23]

The only feasible intellectual solution was to assert that the *aristoi* were still best in *arete,* virtue to be gained by inheritance and by conscious effort; men of this stamp shared "qualities of the inner spirit: superior sensibility and sensitivity, wisdom, grace, and ultimately 'moral' goodness."[24] Theognis expressed this argument, but as a man of mediocre nature himself he portrayed aristocratic life largely in terms of dinners, noble music, and drinking in pleasant conversation. He was an indoorsman uninterested in hunting or "evil war," though he admitted that one must fight for one's *polis.*

Such a solution did not resolve all the troubles which Theognis faced, for he had also to admit that non-aristocratic elements "corrupt the common folk" and reach political office. It was they, in his view, who caused trouble in the state as a consequence, which could lead to internal discord and even to tyranny. In the end Cyrnus seems to have turned away because of their temptations; Theognis cursed him as a chill and wily snake, and urged his readers to be chameleons to all. Theognis was deeply pessimistic and could not provide a conscious answer to the puzzle of earthly injustice, but he still was a Greek in the clarity of his expression and vivid poetic images, facing a world of change, cruel as it was, unafraid: "May I be happy and beloved of the Immortal Gods, Cyrnus, that is the only achievement I desire" (653–654). But in this witness one can best see how far the political mastery of the aristocracy had been weakened.

Another strand of Greek thought led in the same direction, the concept of *to meson*. From Homer on the term is used for "common" or "public" as in the sharing of booty or standing in the middle of the assembly. By the fifth century it often means the whole community; heralds in tragedy proclaim, "Who has wholesome counsel to declare to *to meson?*"; at Athens the law courts met in a spot called Meson.[25] More generally the term *to meson* can be derived from the general Greek principle, "observe due measure," which is voiced in both the *Odyssey* and Hesiod,[26] but by the sixth century the concept takes on a more specific connotation of adopting a stance between conflicting factions, as in a number of Solon's exhortations. More briefly Phocylides proclaims, "Midmost in a *polis* would I be," and Theognis advises, "Walk the road, like me, in the middle."[27] The clearest statement of this wing of thought comes far later in Euripides' *Suppliants,* where three ranks of citizens are distinguished, the rich who seek ever more, the poor who carp at their betters, "while the class that is midmost of the three preserves cities, observing such order as the state ordains."[28]

The term "class" is misleading, for in ancient history there was never a middle class in a modern sense;[29] rather this is a point of view shared by those who disliked factionalism and civil strife— *to meson* is not conceived as a posture between rich and poor, but as a standpoint in the midst of the aristocracy proper. Yet those who preferred moderation sapped the upper-class strength from within at a time when the middling farmers were gaining greater voice. By 500 accordingly most aristocracies had voluntarily or perforce yielded their monopoly so far that the usual form of Greek government can properly be called an oligarchy, that is, a structure in which fundamental decisions were taken by the well-to-do in council and in occupancy of public office; often an assembly was present but only in an advisory capacity. Limitation on membership in the assembly was not often enforced; but as Aristotle observed in treating the oligarchies of his day there was a great variety in practice, based partly on differences in wealth but also on the degree of economic specialization and modes of livelihood.[30] Open divisiveness either on the aristocratic level or between upper and lower orders had been overpassed; when disagreements surfaced in the fifth century, they were largely over foreign policy (i.e., which major state to follow).[31]

The Perfected *Polis*

The years centering on 500 were a period of consolidation and clarification in many aspects of Greek arts and letters, a base on which the fifth century was to build and attain majestic heights. The potters of Athens had advanced from black-figure style to the famous red-figure design about 525 and were creating some of the most magnificent vases ever produced in any society. The last *kore* dedicated on the Acropolis before the Persian sack of 480, the Euthydikos *kore,* displays in its severe, simple lines the first stage of classical sculpture in which the inner structure of the human body harmonizes with its external form to create a unified glorification of mankind. Architects had become masters of the Doric style and were ready to build the temples of Sicily, Olympia, Athens, and elsewhere. Soon Aeschylus was to explore in tragedy the flaws of human imperfection, Pindar to celebrate athletic victory in shimmering odes, and Herodotus to offer an intricately interwoven tale in true historical comprehension.

So too the *polis* by 500 had reached a perfected form with regular rules of procedure and a developed, conscious unity. By this point, moreover, the whole complex of *poleis* had attained a balance which resisted the distortions first of the Persian invasion, then of Athenian imperialism, and in the early fourth century Spartan narrow-minded domination, before it finally was upset by Macedonian conquest.

The Greeks had evolved a system of government in which there could be *citizens* rather than passive auditors of the Homeric *basileis,* and these citizens could have a true voice in shaping policy.[32] Many rural residents were too distant and too busy to attend the assembly often, but its decisions were important; they could lead to war and possible death. Far more than modern voters who choose representatives the Greek citizen was involved directly in the political processes of his community; indeed "the concerns that were primary were not social, they were political."[33]

The achievement was essentially a response evolved over centuries to changing needs in Greek society and values which had to be satisfied politically. As developed by 500 at Athens and in the oligarchies of Hellas, however, conscious organization had been achieved in which the needs of the individual and the demands of the community had been harmonized, as they were in the Euthydikos *kore.* A recent comment on European political development applies equally to the ancient Greek world: "The enjoyment of liberal freedoms is only possible on the basis of a complicated set of restraints and inhibitions, invisible to the naked eye, which constitute the hidden foundations of a liberal society. For liberty is a skill which Europeans have been developing over many centuries."[34]

Still, let us not be carried too far by enthusiasm; human institutions are never without flaws. The most glowing portrayal of the spirit of the *polis* is given in Pericles' Funeral Oration, which celebrates patriotism and communal consensus; but it cannot be taken at face value. Pericles himself admitted that there were citizens unconcerned with public affairs and scorned them as failing in their fundamental duties; it is far from certain that all citizens passionately desired to participate in the government of Athens, or for that matter considered their own merits suitably rewarded in a democracy. A bitter tract by a conservative who is called the Old Oligarch reveals that the well-to-do sometimes felt themselves without proper voice in the conduct of state policy and subject to oppression in the law courts and elsewhere. On a far higher level Sophocles explored in the *Antigone* the conflicting requirements of the imperious *polis* and the inherited, personal religious responsibilities of the individual.

Athens, moreover, exhibits a wider range of public persecution of heretical views than all other Greek states combined. As Burckhardt thoughtfully put it, "The Periclean Age was in every sense of the word an age in which any peaceful and prudent man of our time would refuse to live" by reason of its huge taxes and the inquisitions by demagogues and sycophants. "Yet the Athenians of that age must have felt a plenitude of life which far outweighed any security in the world."[35] The *polis* world also was riven by emphasis on the freedom of the individual small states, jealous and suspicious of each other; it could never be united until the basic spirit of the *polis* had been broken by Philip, Alexander, and eventually the Roman legionaries with their hob-nailed boots.

The *polis,* even so, was a totally new political structure in history; the Greeks had no model either for its initial crystallization in the eighth century or its evolution in response to the great social, economic, and intellectual changes of the succeeding centuries. These challenges were met and very successfully so. Unprecedented, yes, and not without lasting impact in later ages. One might like to end with a flourish and proclaim that the modern Western world directly inherited its concepts of the rights and duties of citizens and of government by due process rather than arbitrary fiat, but this would be to do violence to historical reality. From the Renaissance on men could learn to appreciate Greek literature, rooted in the *polis,* and modern political philosophers have been much indebted to their Greek philosophers; yet in the hurly-burly of actual life the inhabitants of England, France, the United States, and elsewhere had to find their own solutions to their own problems and have fashioned political systems which are far more intricate than those of the *polis* and demand less complete absorption of the citizen in political processes. Even in its own right, nonetheless, the Greek political achievement, beginning from a primitive way of life and thought, is an amazing illustration of the potentialities of mankind.

Notes

Chapter I

1. Pseudo-Dicaearchus, *Fragmenta Historicorum Graecorum*, ed. K. Müller, 2 (Paris, 1878), p. 254.
2. Juliet du Boulay, *Portrait of a Greek Mountain Village* (Oxford, 1974).
3. As, for example, P. Walcot, *Greek Peasants: Ancient and Modern* (Manchester, 1971), or Richard and Eva Blum, *The Dangerous Hour* (New York, 1970). The best study in English of the Greek rural population remains I. T. Sanders, *Rainbow in the Rock* (Cambridge, Mass., 1962).
4. G. A. Megas, *Greek Calendar Customs* (2d ed.; Athens, 1963), p. 39, who emphasizes the continued rural influence on the Greek calendar.
5. Standard works are A. Philippson, *Das Klima Griechenlands* (Bonn, 1948), and *Die griechischen Landschaften,* with E. Kirsten, 3 vols. (Frankfurt, 1950–59). See also E. Kirsten, *Die griechische Polis als historisch-geographisches Problem des Mittelmeerraumes* (Bonn, 1956), and J. L. Myres, *Geographical History in Greek Lands* (Oxford, 1953).
6. C. Vita-Finzi, *The Mediterranean Valleys* (Cambridge, 1969); Peter Shelford discusses plate tectonics in C. Renfrew and M. Wagstaff, edd., *An Island Polity* (Cambridge, 1982), pp. 74–76; on the deforestation of Attica see the reserves of R. Meiggs, *Trees and Timber in the Ancient Mediterranean World* (Oxford, 1982), pp. 188–91.
7. Rhys Carpenter, *Discontinuity in Greek Civilization* (Chicago, 1966), sought to explain the changes of the Dark Ages by alterations in climate, but pollen analysis has not supported his mechanistic interpretation; cf. J. R. A. Turner and J. Turner, "Some Pollen Dia-

grams and Their Archaeological Significance," *Journal of Archaeological Science,* 1 (1974), pp. 177–94; M. Cary, *The Geographic Background of Greek and Roman History* (Oxford, 1949), p. 23.

8. Irrigation at Corinth is briefly discussed by J. Salmon, *Wealthy Corinth* (Oxford, 1962), p. 8; other ancient examples in W. M. Murray, "The Ancient Dam of the Mytikas Valley," *American Journal of Archaeology,* 88 (1984), pp. 199–203.

9. Aristotle, *Politics* 7. 6. 1 1327b; cf. the praises by the sober Philippson of heightened *Lebensgefühl* and *geistige Regsamkeit, Die griechische Landschaften,* 1. 3, p. 779; or Cary, *Geographic Background,* pp. 39, 79. Henry Miller, *The Colossus of Maroussi* (New York, 1941), p. 146, is a typical dithyramb, but then he was sitting in a taverna before the Second World War, not today.

10. Modern comparative statistics are given in my *Economic and Social Growth of Early Greece, 800–500 B.C.* (New York, 1977), pp. 152–53, a work on which I have drawn here.

11. E. Ruschenbusch, *Solonos Nomoi (Historia,* Einzelschrift 9; 1966), F 89.

12. Sanders, *Rainbow,* p. 88.

13. J. M. Frayn, *Subsistence Farming in Roman Italy* (Fontwell, Sussex, 1979), c. 4.

14. *Economic and Social Growth of Early Greece,* pp. 153–54; *Island Polity,* pp. 106, 117.

15. *Island Polity,* p. 110; Michael Chisholm, *Rural Settlement and Land Use* (London, 1968), pp. 50ff.

16. *Economic and Social Growth of Early Greece,* pp. 41–42, with references; Solon fr. 19.

17. Cf. *Iliad* 3. 108ff., 4. 324 on role of elders; Athenaeus 15. 693ff.; Mimnermus frr. 6, 9 against Solon fr. 22. In general, B. E. Richardson, *Old Age among the Ancient Greeks* (Baltimore, 1933).

18. *Works and Days* 376ff. A. Zimmern, *The Greek Commonwealth* (Oxford paperback, 1961), pp. 326ff., comments on the stagnation of the Greek population for both deliberate and unintentional reasons.

19. H. Bolkestein, *Economic Life in Greece's Golden Age* (Leiden, 1958), p. 6.

20. *Iliad* 1. 481–83, 4. 422ff.

21. Cary, *Geographic Background,* p. 45.

22. *Works and Days* 691. Cf. *Odyssey* 1. 162, 15. 344, 23. 269ff. on the desirability of staying home and the dangers of the sea.

23. Thucydides 1. 7; my essay, "Minoan Flower Lovers," *The Minoan*

Thalassocracy, ed. Robin Hägg and Nanno Marinatos (Stockholm, 1984), pp. 9–12.

24. Thucydides 1 init., 2. 60–64; my "Thucydides on Sea Power," *Mnemosyne,* 31 (1979), pp. 343–50. Against Mahan's pervasive influence one must always set Sir Halford Mackinder's emphasis on land power in *Democratic Ideals and Reality* (London, 1919).

25. See N. K. Sanders, *The Sea Peoples* (New York, 1979); E. Craik, *The Dorian Aegean* (London, 1980), a potpourri of information not always well assessed; *Griechenland, die Ägäis und die Levante während der "Dark Ages" vom 12. bis zum 9. Jahrhundert v. Chr.,* ed. S. Deger-Jalkotzy (Vienna, 1983).

26. C. M. Woodhouse, *Karamanlis: The Restorer of Greek Democracy* (Oxford, 1982), pp. 275, 90–91.

27. Herodotus 7. 102. *Penia,* it should be noted, means the necessity of physical labor, not the grinding hardship of the *ptochos* (beggar).

28. G. E. M. de Ste Croix, "The Estate of Phaenippus," *Ancient Society and Institutions* (Oxford, 1966), pp. 109–14.

29. *Politics* 1. 1. 9 1253a; much the same definition is in *Nicomachean Ethics* 9. 9. 3 1169b.

Chapter II

1. An approach has been sketched in my *Origins of Greek Civilization, 1100–650 B.C.* (New York, 1961) and more briefly in "La storia greca arcaica," *Rivista di filologia,* 92 (1964), pp. 2–23 (now in *Essays on Ancient History* [Leiden, 1979], pp. 103–21).

2. A. Snodgrass, "Two Demographic Notes," *The Greek Renaissance of the Eighth Century B.C.,* ed. Robin Hägg (Stockholm, 1983), pp. 167–71.

3. *Archaeological Reports for 1981–82,* pp. 16–17; *for 1982–83,* p. 13. Early houses have been found at Asine, S. Dietz, *Asine,* 2 (Stockholm, 1982).

4. G. S. Kirk, *Cambridge Ancient History,* 2. 2 (3d ed.; Cambridge, 1974), pp. 820–50, is a solid survey of the Homeric poems as history; M. L. West has sought to put Hesiod before Homer, but most students rightly keep the traditional order. See F. Solmsen, *Hesiod and Aeschylus* (Ithaca, 1949).

5. A. M. Snodgrass, "An Historical Homeric Society?" *Journal of Hellenic Studies,* 94 (1974), pp. 114–25, raises difficult problems, partly in disagreement with M. I. Finley, *The World of Odysseus* (rev. ed.; New York, 1979), which is nonetheless a valuable study,

and with A. W. H. Adkins, "Homeric Values and Homeric Society," *Journal of Hellenic Studies,* 91 (1971), pp. 1–14; but O. Murray, *Early Greece* (Atlantic Highlands, N.J., 1980), p. 42, points out that bride-price and dowry do coexist in historical societies. In *Moral Values and Political Behaviour in Ancient Greece* (New York, 1974), p. 10, Adkins sticks to his views.

6. Max Gluckman, *Politics, Law and Ritual in Tribal Society* (Oxford, 1964), p. xv. In "Reciprocities in Homer," *Classical World,* 75 (1982), pp. 137–74, and other essays W. Donlan makes good use of anthropological theory in considering the epic world.

7. M. Sahlins, *Tribesmen* (Englewood Cliffs, N.J., 1968), pp. 91–93.

8. J. Haas, *The Evolution of the Prehistoric State* (New York, 1982), p. 10.

9. On the much debated question of Homeric kingship see recently J. V. Andreev, "Könige und Königsherrschaft in den Epen Homer," *Klio,* 61 (1979), pp. 368–84; R. Descat, "L'Idéologie homérique du pouvoir," *Revue des études anciennes,* 81 (1979), pp. 229–40; B. Qviller, "The Dynamics of the Homeric Society," *Symbolae Osloenses,* 56 (1981), pp. 109–55; R. Drews, *Basileus* (New Haven, 1983). A. Fanta, *Der Staat in der Ilias und Odyssee* (Innsbruck, 1882), remains useful. On the assembly cf. also J. V. Andreev, "Die politischen Funktionen der Volkssammlung im homerischen Zeitalter," *Klio,* 61 (1979), pp. 385–406.

10. To avoid a plethora of notes I shall usually give citations to the *Iliad* and *Odyssey* by book and lines in the text; the translations are as a rule those of W. H. D. Rouse, which well reproduce the vigorous but not yet refined quality of Homeric Greek. For text I rely on the Oxford editions.

11. 19. 40ff. The line quoted was omitted by Zenodotus, but A. T. Murray (Loeb translation) justifies its retention.

12. F. J. M. de Waele, *The Magic Staff or Rod in Graeco-Italian Antiquity* (Ghent, 1927).

13. 2. 394, 7. 403–04, 8. 542, 9. 50, 18. 310. On Thersites see W. Donlan, *The Aristocratic Ideal in Archaic Greece* (Lawrence, Kans., 1980), pp. 20–21, who points out that he had spoken on other occasions; H. D. Rankin, "Thersites the Malcontent, A Discussion," *Symbolae Osloenses,* 47 (1972), pp. 36–60.

14. I. Schapera, *Tribal Legislation among the Tswana of the Bechuanaland Protectorate* (London, 1943).

15. It is true that in 15. 532 another *basileus* is called *anax,* and the word appears fairly often as a verb.

16. 7. 274ff. Cf. the French and English heralds at Agincourt who decided which side had won and how the battle should be named (J. Keegan, *The Face of Battle* [London, 1971], p. 112). Skulker: 23. 91, quoted by Aristotle, *Politics* 3. 9. 2 1285a.

17. H. H. Pflüger, "Die Gerichtszene auf den Schilde des Achilleus," *Hermes,* 77 (1942), pp. 140–48; R. J. Bonner and G. Smith, *The Administration of Justice from Homer to Aristotle,* 1 (Chicago, 1930), c. 1.

18. Snodgrass, *Journal of Hellenic Studies,* 94 (1974), p. 124.

19. In *Iliad* 17. 250 and *Odyssey* 1. 226 the meals (*eranoi*) are met by joint contributions.

20. As Donlan, *Parola del Passato,* 25 (1970), p. 383, notes, the term *demos* sometimes, but not often, means *all* the population of an area.

21. In my "Homeric Cowards and Heroes," *The Classical Tradition,* ed. L. Wallach (Ithaca, 1964), pp. 48–63 (now in my *Essays on Ancient History,* pp. 97–102) I have noted that in the Song of Roland personal combat is emphasized whereas in Frankish chronicles the warriors fought in tight tactical units. G. S. Kirk, *Problèmes de la guerre en Grèce ancienne,* ed. J. P. Vernant (Paris, 1968), pp. 110–12, also stresses that Homeric duels are "a poetical device."

22. Yet Homer also has similes to the boy who plays in the sand by the sea (15. 362) or the baby girl who begs her mother to pick her up (16. 10).

23. See recently C. G. Thomas, "Homer and the Polis," *Parola del Passato,* 21 (1966), pp. 5–14; F. Gschnitzer, "Stadt und Stamm bei Homer," *Chiron,* 1 (1971), pp. 1–17; R. H. Simpson and J. F. Lazenby, *The Catalogue of Ships in Homer's Iliad* (Oxford, 1970), a judicious analysis of the difficulties of matching this geographical description with *any* period of Greek history.

24. *Odyssey* 14. 187, 15. 264, 24. 298.

25. A point well made by P. Rahe, *American Historical Review,* 89 (1984), pp. 275–76, citing *Politics* 1. 1. 9 1253a (just after Aristotle's famous definition of man as a political animal).

26. *Odyssey* 13. 201–02 and elsewhere; Thucydides 1. 2 postulates ease of migration in early times; Euripides, *Phoenician Women* 385ff., gives a more bitter picture of exiles in classical times. Craftsmen, to be sure, always remained in an ambiguous position in social acceptance (Murray, *Early Greece,* pp. 58, 210–11; A. Burford, *Craftsmen in Greek and Roman Society* [London, 1972]).

27. A. Lesky, *A History of Greek Literature* (New York, 1966), pp. 68–

70; H. Lloyd-Jones, *The Justice of Zeus* (2d ed.; Berkeley, 1983), pp. 28ff.

28. *Works and Days* 217ff., 254–55 (= 124–35); M. Gagarin, *"Dike* in the *Works and Days,"* *Classical Philology,* 68 (1973), pp. 81–94, goes too far in restricting the meaning of *dike* here; see M. W. Dickie, *"Dike* as a Moral Term in Homer and Hesiod," *Classical Philology,* 73 (1978), pp. 96–99.

29. *Cherees* (meaner) and *agathos* are, however, also distinguished in 15. 324; *esthles* and *chereia* in 18. 229, 20. 310; *kakon* and *esthlos* in *Iliad* 6. 489 and *Odyssey* 22. 415, but these terms, as also *aristos,* are not yet sharply defined.

30. P. W. Rose, "Class Ambivalence in the *Odyssey," Historia,* 24 (1974), pp. 129–49; see also F. Gschnitzer, "Politische Leidenschaft im homerischen Epos," *Studien zum antiken Epos,* ed. H. Görgemanns and E. A. Schmidt (Meissenheim, 1976), pp. 1–21.

31. Two valuable essays are by H. Strasburger, "Der soziologische Aspekt der homerischen Epen," *Gymnasium,* 60 (1953), pp. 97–114, and "Der Einzelne und die Gemeinschaft im Denken der Griechen," *Historische Zeitschrift,* 177 (1954), pp. 227–48 (now in his *Studien zur Alten Geschichte,* 1 [Hildesheim, 1982], pp. 491–518, 423–48).

32. C. Meier, *Die Entstehung des Politischen bei den Griechen* (Frankfurt, 1980), p. 269; W. K. Lacey, *The Family in Classical Greece* (London, 1968), p. 9, observes that there is "scarcely any topic in Greek civilization in which the family is not concerned."

33. "Homeric Cowards and Heroes," p. 61; *Iliad* 12. 243, 15. 496–98, 15. 662ff. P. A. L. Greenhalgh, "Patriotism in the Homeric World," *Historia,* 21 (1972), pp. 528–37.

34. H. Strasburger, "Zum antiken Gesellschaftsideal," *Abhandlungen der Heidelberger Akademie der Wissenschaft,* phil.-hist. K1 (1975), p. 22.

35. A. R. W. Harrison, *The Law of Athens* (Oxford, 1968), pp. 132ff.; J. A. Newth in Molly Miller, *The Sicilian Colony Dates* (Albany, 1970), pp. 133ff.; D. Henning, "Grundbesitz bei Homer und Hesiod," *Chiron,* 10 (1980), pp. 35–52; my *Economic and Social Growth of Early Greece,* pp. 150–51, with citations. The opposite view is stated by E. Will, "Aux origines du régime foncièr grec," *Revue des études anciennes,* 59 (1957), pp. 5–50.

36. The role of *symposia* is properly stressed by O. Murray, *Renaissance of the Eighth Century,* pp. 195–99; on phratries see A. Andrewes, "Phratries in Homer," *Hermes,* 89 (1961), pp. 129–40.

37. *Iliad* 20. 252ff. Du Boulay, *Mountain Village,* p. 102, observes the

basic irresponsibility of women (in male eyes) in their gossip today.

38. D. Schaps, *The Economic Rights of Women in Ancient Greece* (Edinburgh, 1979); Gluckman, *Politics,* pp. 224–26, 248–49, has an interesting collection of views of women as "evil in their very nature" in many primitive societies; cf. J. P. Gould, "Law, Custom and Myth," *Journal of Hellenic Studies,* 100 (1980), pp. 38–59.

39. F. Bourriot, *Recherches sur la nature du genos* (Paris, 1976); see also D. Roussel, *Tribu et cité* (Paris, 1976).

40. Finley, *World of Odysseus,* p. 105 (but earlier he discusses at length the ties of kinship, largely in household terms). Sally Humphreys, *Anthropology and the Greeks* (London, 1978), would still like to stress kinship but admits (p. 198), "political procedures developed in Greece at the expense of kinship"; R. J. Littman, "Kinship in Athens," *Ancient Society,* 10 (1979), pp. 5–31, goes much further in evaluating the public importance of kinship.

41. Cf. J. P. Vernant, "Le mariage en Grèce archaïque," *Parola del Passato,* 28 (1974), pp. 51–74; Hesiod, *Works and Days,* 702–04.

42. A. W. H. Adkins, *Merit and Responsibility* (Oxford, 1960), p. 34.

43. I have noted this problem at greater length in *Economic and Social Growth of Early Greece,* pp. 119ff., a discussion abbreviated here.

44. The gibe of Phocylides fr. 3, "Of what advantage is high birth to such as have no grace either in words or in council?" serves as adequate illustration; but it may be noted that throughout Trollope's novels a gentleman is one by birth and cannot be made such (cf. the dubious position and character of Lopez in *The Prime Minister,* which leads to his downfall).

45. *Iliad* 18. 106, 252; in 3. 212 Menelaus is thus contrasted with Odysseus; cf. also 1. 490, 3. 150, 9. 441.

46. M. I. Finley, "The World of Odysseus Revisited," *Proceedings of the Classical Association,* 71 (1974), pp. 13–31, defends his emphasis on gift exchange in *The World of Odysseus* and elsewhere; Snodgrass, *Journal of Hellenic Studies,* 94 (1974), p. 124, is dubious as are others. J. N. Coldstream, "Gift Exchange in the Eighth Century B.C.," *Renaissance of the Eighth Century,* pp. 201–06, seeks to find actual examples in vases of the era.

47. W. Donlan, "The Homeric Economy," *American Journal of Ancient History,* 6 (1981), pp. 101–17, is a very full list of all gifts in the epics.

48. *Iliad* 21. 450ff.; in *Odyssey* 10. 84 double wage is earned by working day and night; see also 18. 358.

49. Nestor in *Iliad* 9. 63.
50. H. J. Rose, *Primitive Culture in Greece* (London, 1925), pp. 109–33; *Supplementum Epigraphicum Graecum* 9. 1 (Leiden, 1938), no. 72, on the rules at Cyrene in the early fourth century.
51. R. F. Willetts, *Cambridge Ancient History,* 3. 3, p. 235, summing up J. W. Headlam, *Journal of Hellenic Studies,* 13 (1892/3), pp. 48–69; in *Aristocratic Society in Ancient Crete* (London, 1955), Willetts illustrates the survivals of earlier customs on Crete.

Chapter III

1. So Terpander at Sparta (J. M. Edmonds, *Lyra Graeca,* 2 [Cambridge, 1924], p. 68, quoting Philodemus, *Mus.* p. 87K): Anacreon and Simonides at Athens (Ps-Plato, *Hipparchus* 228).
2. 30ff., in 216ff. Apollo essentially rules over states.
3. J. M. Cook, *Cambridge Ancient History,* 2. 2, p. 804; C. J. Emlyn-Jones, *The Ionians and Hellenism* (London, 1980).
4. A. M. Snodgrass, *Arms and Armour of the Greeks* (London, 1967), p. 46. The physical evidence is discussed in G. Ahlberg, *Fighting on Land and Sea in Greek Geometric Art* (Stockholm, 1971) and P. A. L. Greenhalgh, *Early Greek Warfare* (Cambridge, 1973). Karl von Clausewitz, *On War,* trans. M. Howard and P. Paret (Princeton, 1976), p. 75.
5. An earlier date was advanced by V. Ehrenberg, "When Did the Polis Arise?" *Journal of Hellenic Studies,* 57 (1937), pp. 147–59. A. Snodgrass, *Archaic Greece* (London, 1980), pp. 32–33 and F. Gschnitzer, *Griechische Sozialgeschichte von der mykenischen bis zum Ausgang der klassischen Zeit* (Wiesbaden, 1981), pp. 42–43, prefer the eighth century; see also my essay, "The Early Greek City-State," *Parola del Passato,* 12 (1957), pp. 97–108 (now in *Essays on Ancient History,* pp. 122–33).
6. Rahe, *American Historical Review,* 89 (1984), p. 269 n. 9, citing H. C. Mansfield Jr., "On the Impersonality of the Modern State," *American Political Science Review,* 77 (1983), pp. 849–57.
7. Snodgrass, *Archaic Greece,* p. 28, gives as two major characteristics the political independence and the unity of the main settlement in a *polis* and its countryside. Also useful are C. Renfrew, *The Emergence of Civilisation* (London, 1972); W. G. Runciman, "Origins of States: The Case of Archaic Greece," *Comparative Studies in Society and History,* 24 (1982), pp. 351–77. Interesting parallels from Italian development may be found in J. C. Meyer, *Pre-Republican*

Rome (Odense, 1983), pp. 94–95, and G. Barker, *Landscape and Society* (London, 1981).

8. Alcaeus fr. Z 103; or more briefly Thucydides 7. 77, "men are the *polis.*"

9. Herodotus 8. 61; V. Ehrenberg, *From Solon to Socrates* (London, 1968), p. 7.

10. See recently F. Prinz, *Gründungsmythen und Sagenchronologie* (Munich, 1979); my *Origins of Greek Civilization,* pp. 156ff.

11. A. M. Snodgrass, "The Formation of the Greek City-State," *Proceedings of the Classical Association,* 79 (1982), pp. 27–28.

12. Snodgrass, *Archaic Greece,* pp. 35–40, and Murray, *Early Greece,* pp. 46–47, have argued for this change; earlier T. P. Howe, *Transactions of the American Philological Association,* 89 (1958), pp. 44–65, had advanced the same view, but her reading of the epic and Hesiodic evidence is not compelling.

13. J. McK. Camp II, "A Drought in the Late Eighth Century B.C.," *Hesperia,* 48 (1979), pp. 397–411; countered by Snodgrass, *Renaissance of the Eighth Century,* pp. 169–71, in keeping with his fuller analysis in *Archaic Greece,* pp. 19–25, and *Cambridge Ancient History,* 3. 1, pp. 687, 668–69. S. Dietz, *Asine,* 2 (Stockholm), also finds a dramatic increase in population at that site, and R. J. Buck, *A History of Boeotia* (Edmonton, 1979), pp. 81, 87, counts a steady increase in settlements on the Boeotian plain.

14. E. Kirsten in Philippson, *Die griechischen Landschaften,* 1. 3, p. 994; cf. A. Andrewes, *Cambridge Ancient History,* 3. 3, p. 380. T. W. Gallant, "Agricultural Systems, Land Tenure and the Reforms of Solon," *Annual of the British School at Athens,* 77 (1982), pp. 111–24, discusses changes in agricultural organization.

15. M. L. Hansen, *The Atlantic Migration (1607–1860)* (Cambridge, Mass., 1945), remains a provocative study; see more recently P. Taylor, *The Distant Magnet* (London, 1971). Murray, *Early Greece,* p. 110, suggests that usually a body of Greek colonists numbered 200 or less.

16. M. Sahlins, *Stone Age Economics* (London, 1972), p. 49.

17. E. Boserup, *The Conditions of Agricultural Growth* (Chicago, 1965).

18. Salmon, *Wealthy Corinth,* pp. 67–70, continues the unbelievable picture of a wide range of allies in this struggle; S. D. Lambert, *Journal of Hellenic Studies,* 102 (1982), pp. 216–20, properly urges caution in interpreting Thucydides 1. 15 as proving that this was a general war (he thus cites the scolion on Thucydides, "alone the Chalcidians fought the Eretrians").

19. R. P. Legon, *Megara* (Ithaca, 1981), pp. 59–70, accepts this Corinthian expansion; Salmon, *Wealthy Corinth*, p. 71, is brief and muffled. The information about Orsippus comes from *Inscriptiones Graecae* 7. 52, as expanded by Pausanias 1. 44. 1; according to Pausanias 6. 19. 12–14 the Megarians early built a treasury at Olympia from Corinthian spoils, presumably in this war.

20. J. N. Coldstream, *Geometric Greece* (London, 1979), pp. 317–19, lists at least 70 places of worship known by 700, nearly half with temples; this list can be expanded. He describes (pp. 278–79) an *agora* at Dreros of this period, with a flight of steps along the side of a flat rectangular expanse; but J. Boardman, *Cambridge Ancient History*, 3. 3, p. 445, has reserves on ascribing significance to the existence of an *agora*. R. Hägg, in *Palast und Hütte*, ed. D. Papenfuss and V. M. Strocka (Mainz, 1982), would not date the civic center of Asine before 700–675.

21. *Athenaion Politeia* 43. 6.

22. F. Sokolowski, *Lois sacrées des cités grecques* (Paris, 1969), no. 110; cf. the effort to exclude Cleomenes from the Acropolis at Athens (Herodotus 5. 72. 3) and the rule in Aristotle, *Politics* 7. 8. 6 1329a, that only citizens can worship the gods. F. Böhringer, "Mégare: traditions mythiques, espace sacré et naissance de la cité," *L'Antiquité classique*, 49 (1980), pp. 5–22, also stresses the intimate tie of *polis* and religion.

23. E. Badian, *Publicans and Sinners* (Ithaca, 1972), p. 14; G. Rudé, *Europe in the Eighteenth Century* (London, 1972), p. 103.

24. R. Felsch, *Renaissance of the Eighth Century*, pp. 123–29, and K. Killian, pp. 131–46; *Archaeological Reports for 1982–83*, p. 18; T. J. Dunbabin, *Perachora*, 2 (Oxford, 1962), pp. 528–29, who also cites evidence for potters and metalworkers at Delos, figurine makers at Acragas etc. Snodgrass, *Archaic Greece*, pp. 52–53, lists metal dedications at sanctuaries but not the workshops.

25. Renfrew, *Emergence of Civilisation*, pp. 320ff.; Snodgrass, *Archaic Greece*, pp. 49ff.; Meyer, *Pre-Republican Rome*, pp. 98–99.

26. *Renaissance of the Eighth Century*, p. 195.

27. R. Hägg, "Burial Customs and Social Differentiation in 8th Century Argos," *Renaissance of the Eighth Century*, pp. 27–31, is the latest discussion of this topic; see also the list of sites by C. Sourvinou-Inwood, p. 44, and generally D. C. Kurtz and J. Boardman, *Greek Burial Customs* (Ithaca, 1971).

28. Meyer, *Pre-Republican Rome*, pp. 96–97.

29. Dio Chrysostom, *Orations* 36.5; the most recent survey of colonization is A. J. Graham, *Cambridge Ancient History*, 3. 3, pp. 83ff.

30. R. Drews, "Phoenicians, Carthage and the Spartan *Eunomia*," *American Journal of Philology*, 100 (1979), pp. 45–58, defends Phoenician influence, which has been suggested in passing by others (e.g., Snodgrass, *Archaic Greece*, pp. 31–32).

31. T. F. R. G. Braun, *Cambridge Ancient History*, 3. 3, p. 28; and O. Szemerényi, *Journal of Hellenic Studies*, 94 (1974), pp. 147–52.

32. Lawrence Stone, *Past and Present*, no. 85 (1979), pp. 13–14.

33. Sahlins, *Tribesmen*, p. 24.

34. Haas, *Evolution of the Prehistoric State*, pp. 47–49 (from M. H. Fried, *The Evolution of Political Society* [New York, 1967], pp. 109, 278, 238). Renfrew, *Island Polity*, pp. 281ff., applies what may be termed the Friedian model to Melos.

35. E. R. Service, *Origins of the State and Civilization* (Philadelphia, 1978), p. 8; Haas, p. 20.

36. *From Max Weber: Essays in Sociology* (New York, 1946), p. 78, quoted by Rahe, *American Historical Review*, 89 (1984), p. 268.

37. So even the sober Busolt, *Griechische Staatskunde*, 1, pp. 210ff. As A. Lintott, *Violence, Civil Strife and Revolution in the Classical City 750–330 B.C.* (London, 1982), p. 257, points out, the lack of a labor market as such and of a split between employer and employee makes Marxist views less relevant to ancient Greek economic life.

38. W. G. Forrest, *The Emergence of Greek Democracy* (London, 1966), pp. 55–58.

39. *Politics in the Ancient World* (Cambridge, 1983), pp. 2, 131.

40. H. Kissinger, *Years of Upheaval* (Boston, 1982), p. 735.

41. *Politics* 4. 9. 6 1295b; 3. 5. 11 1280b; also in *Nicomachean Ethics* 8. 12 1161b; 8. 9 1160a.

42. C. Beard, *An Economic Interpretation of the Constitution of the United States* (New York, 1913); E. M. and N. Wood, *Class Ideology and Ancient Political Theory* (Oxford, 1978).

43. J. Gottmann, *The Significance of Territory* (Charlottesville, 1973), has interesting comments on the psychological as well as geographical forces which can lead a state to desire to remain small in population and area; both Montesquieu and Hume favored small states for similar reasons (T. Draper, *Encounter*, February 1982), pp. 34–47. See also D. Friedman, "A Theory of the Size and Shape of Nations," *Journal of Political Economy*, 85 (1977), pp. 59–77.

44. E. Ruschenbusch, *Untersuchungen zu Staat und Politik in Griechen-*

land vom 7.–4. Jh v. Chr. (Bamberg, 1978), pp. 4ff.; N. J. G. Pounds, "The Urbanization of the Classical World," *Annals of the Association of American Geographers,* 59 (1969), pp. 135–57.

45. Ruschenbusch, pp. 4–12, 19; Aristotle, *Politics* 4. 12. 5 1299b.

46. H. P. Drögemüller, *Syrakus* (*Gymnasium* Beiheft 6, 1969), p. 97; Salmon, *Wealthy Corinth,* p. 168; Cook, *Cambridge Ancient History,* 3. 3., p. 218; my *Economic and Social Growth of Early Greece,* pp. 152–56. If Aegina could man 30 triremes in the Persian wars from its own manpower, it had a much larger population than the island does noways (Murray, *Early Greece,* pp. 211–12). J. Beloch, *Die Bevölkerung der griechisch-römischen Welt* (Leipzig, 1886), remains valuable.

47. N. J. Richardson, *The Homeric Hymn to Demeter* (Oxford, 1974), pp. 7–11.

48. Plutarch, *Theseus* 24; C. Hignett, *A History of the Athenian Constitution to the End of the Fifth Century B.C.* (Oxford, 1952), pp. 34–35, properly calls the unification a *sympoliteia; synoikismos* entails the concentration of the population in one center. On the elaboration of Theseus see H. Herter, "Theseus," *Rheinisches Museum,* 85 (1936), 88 (1939); W. R. Connor in A. G. Ward ed., *Quest for Theseus* (New York, 1970), pp. 143–74.

49. Andrewes, *Cambridge Ancient History,* 3. 3, p. 362; P. Musiolek, "Zur Begriff und zur Bedeutung des Synoikismos," *Klio,* 63 (1981), pp. 207–13; R. A. Padgug, "Eleusis and the Union of Attica," *Greek, Roman and Byzantine Studies,* 13 (1972), pp. 135–50; C. G. Thomas, "Theseus and Synoicism," *Studi micenei ed Egeo-Anatolici,* 23 (1982), pp. 337–49; S. Diamant, *Hesperia,* Supplement 19 (1982), pp. 38–47, finds economic causes; the festival is discussed in H. W. Parke, *Festivals of the Athenians* (Ithaca, 1979), pp. 31–33. Regionalism: R. Sealey, *Historia,* 9 (1960), pp. 155–80; Busolt, *Griechische Staatskunde,* 2, pp. 773–76.

50. In "The Credibility of Early Spartan History," *Historia,* 14 (1965), pp. 257–72 (*Essays on Ancient History,* pp. 144–59) I have commented on sources and bibliography down to that date. Sparta continues to fascinate modern scholars; in English the best study to this point is W. G. Forrest, *A History of Sparta, 950–192 B.C.* (Norton paperback, 1969).

51. Buck, *History of Boeotia,* pp. 97–98.

52. T. Kelly, "The Argive Destruction of Asine," *Historia,* 16 (1967), pp. 422–31; N. G. L. Hammond, *Cambridge Ancient History,* 3. 3, pp. 326–27.

53. Buck, *History of Boeotia,* pp. 113, 123.
54. Strabo 8. 370; Archilochus fr. 97; Herodotus 8. 144 gives the most famous expression of the sense of Hellenic unity; J. N. Coldstream, "The Meaning of the Regional Styles in the Eighth Century B.C.," *Renaissance of the Eighth Century,* pp. 17–25.
55. T. Kelly, "The Calaurian Amphictiony," *American Journal of Archaeology,* 70 (1966), pp. 113–21; the Panionium did not exist until after the seventh century (Cook, *Cambridge Ancient History,* 3. 1, p. 750, 3. 3, p. 217).
56. Aeschines 2. 115; Cleisthenes of Sicyon was said to have poisoned the water supply of Crisa (Frontinus, *Strategems* 3. 7. 6). See W. G. Forrest, "The First Sacred War," *Bulletin de correspondance hellénique,* 80 (1956), pp. 33–52.
57. V. Martin, *La vie internationale dans la Grèce des cités* (Paris, 1940); Plato, *Laws* 626a.

Chapter IV

1. Mimnermus fr. 7; Phocylides fr. 5 and later Anacreon fr. 59 repeat the theme. Du Boulay, *Mountain Village,* pp. 181–82, 200–11, comments on the role of gossip as enforcing conformity to the accepted values of society; as villagers often say, "You can't shut the mouth of the community" (p. 157).
2. In *Origins of Greek Civilization,* pp. 277ff., I have suggested some of the physical evidence of stress and fear in the era, as marked by the appearance of monsters and death-dealing beasts on vases; E. R. Dodds, *The Greeks and the Irrational* (Beacon paperback, 1957), is a justly famous treatment of the psychological and religious tensions and their solutions.
3. Bolkestein, *Economic Life,* pp. 140–41; W. Kendrick Pritchett, *Ancient Greek Military Practices,* 1 (Berkeley, 1971), pp. 93–100; Ruschenbusch, *Untersuchungen,* pp. 11, 67ff., considers war or its avoidance the *only* subject of foreign policy. On its causes, D. Loenen, *Polemos* (Amsterdam, 1953); on diplomacy, most visible from the fifth century on, F. E. Adcock and D. J. Mosley, *Diplomacy in Ancient Greece* (London, 1975); D. J. Mosley, *Envoys and Diplomacy in Ancient Greece* (*Historia* Einzelschrift 22, 1973); and my *Political Intelligence in Classical Greece* (*Mnemosyne* Supplement 31, 1974).
4. Ruschenbusch, *Solonos Nomoi,* F 76a, gives a law ascribed to Solon which mentions official booty-purchasers.

5. On this much discussed topic see recently A. M. Snodgrass, *Arms and Armour of the Greeks* (London, 1967), and "The Hoplite Reform and History," *Journal of Hellenic Studies,* 85 (1965), pp. 110–22; J. Salmon, "Political Hoplites?" *Journal of Hellenic Studies,* 97 (1977), pp. 84–101; and in the same issue P. Cartledge, "Hoplites and Heroes," pp. 10–27; Y. Garlan, *War in the Ancient World* (New York, 1975).

6. Aristotle, *Politics* 4. 10. 10 1297b.

7. A. J. Podlecki, *The Early Greek Poets and Their Times* (Vancouver, 1984), p. 55, detects in Callinus an emphasis "on the soldier's duty to his civilian community." I wish that I could go so far.

8. W. Jaeger, *Paideia,* 1 (Berlin, 1936), pp. 125ff.; with whom Lloyd-Jones, *Justice of Zeus,* p. 45, disagrees to some extent; Lesky, *History of Greek Literature,* pp. 118–20.

9. *Life of Lycurgus* 6; there is a small difficulty in the Greek text which does not affect the general sense. R. Sealey, *History of the Greek City States ca. 700–338 B.C.* (Berkeley, 1976), pp. 74–78, is the latest scholar to think it a forgery (as earlier E. Meyer); but Andrewes and others properly concur in accepting it.

10. A. Andrewes, *Probouleusis* (Oxford, 1952); D. Butler, "Competence of the Demos in the Spartan Rhetra," *Historia,* 11 (1962), pp. 385–96; V. Ehrenberg, "Der Damos in archaischen Sparta," *Hermes,* 68 (1933), pp. 288–305; K. W. Welwei, "Die spartanische Phylenordnung," *Gymnasium,* 86 (1979), pp. 178–96.

11. W. Donlan, "Changes and Shifts in the Meaning of Demos in the Literature of the Archaic Period," *Parola del Passato,* 25 (1970), pp. 381–95.

12. Herodotus 5. 71; Thucydides 1. 126; Andrewes, *Cambridge Ancient History,* 3. 3, pp. 369–70. Perhaps the most significant evidence for naucraries is the fact that a later coastal deme, Colias, had earlier been a naucrary (I. Bekker, *Anecdota Graeca,* 1 [Berlin, 1814], 275. 20); see B. Jordan, *The Athenian Navy in the Classical Period* (Berkeley, 1975), pp. 9–10. R. Thomsen, *Eisphora* (Copenhagen, 1965), pp. 116–46, considers them personal units for financial purposes, but *Athenaion Politeia* 21. 5 is clear that demes replaced naucraries.

13. *Archaic Greece,* pp. 160–61.

14. See recently Gigante, *Nomos Basileus;* K. Latte, "Der Rechtsgedanke im archaischen Griechentum," *Antike und Abendland,* 2 (1946), pp. 63–76; E. A. Havelock, *The Greek Concept of Justice* (Cambridge, Mass., 1971); Lloyd-Jones, *Justice of Zeus.*

15. Archilochus fr. 230; Willetts, *Cambridge Ancient History*, 3. 3, pp. 234–48; V. Ehrenberg, "An Early Source of Polis Constitution," *Classical Quarterly*, 37 (1943), pp. 14–18.

16. Aristotle, *Politics* 2. 3. 7 1265b, 2. 9. 7 1274a; in nineteenth-century Norway and Germany individual farmers sought privately but with determination to maintain their plots within a system of equal partition (P. Taylor, *The Distant Magnet* [London, 1971], pp. 29, 38).

17. Willetts, *Cambridge Ancient History*, 3. 3, p. 236; M. Mühl, "Die Gesetze des Zaleukos und Charondas," *Klio*, 22 (1928–9), pp. 105–24, 432–63; R. van Compernolle, "La législation aristocratique de Locres Epizéphirene dite législation de Zaleucus," *Antiquité Classique*, 59 (1981), pp. 759–69; G. de Sanctis, *Storia dei Greci*, 1 (Florence, 1939), pp. 468–69, considered him a myth, as have many others.

18. G. E. Lloyd, *Science, Folklore, Ideology* (Cambridge paperback, 1983), pp. 115, 202, after J. Goody, *The Domestication of the Savage Mind* (Cambridge, 1977); A. Johnston, "The Extent and Use of Literacy," *Renaissance of the Eighth Century*, pp. 63–68, gives the latest bibliography on the adoption of the Greek alphabet.

19. Alcaeus Z 59; Phocylides fr. 4; Dionysius of Halicarnassus 1. 89. 4.

20. B. Bergquist, *The Archaic Greek Temenos* (Lund, 1967); J. J. Coulton, *Greek Architects at Work* (London, 1977), pp. 18–22; Salmon, *Wealthy Corinth*, pp. 120–22, assembles the evidence on Corinthian rooftiles.

21. A. Andreades, *A History of Greek Public Finance*, 1 (Cambridge, Mass., 1933), p. 230; a sixth-century law on sacred utensils survives from Argos, *Supplementum Epigraphicum Graecum* 11 (Leiden, 1950), no. 314; my forthcoming essay "Greek Administration," *Civilization of the Ancient Mediterranean*, ed. M. Grant and R. Kitzinger, surveys a much neglected area.

22. C. Rolley, *Renaissance of the Eighth Century*, pp. 109–10, dates the inception of worship at Olympia to the tenth century and at Delphi to the end of the ninth; but there is general agreement that the role of Delphi became extensive only in the seventh century; see W. G. Forrest, "Colonization and the Rise of Delphi," *Historia*, 6 (1957), pp. 160–75, and *Cambridge Ancient History*, 3. 3, p. 311.

23. G. Pugliese Carratelli, *Atti e memoria della società Magna Grecia*, n. s. 6 (1965), pp. 13–17.

24. In my description of the aristocratic way of life I have drawn on the fuller discussion, with more extensive references, in *Economic and Social Growth of Early Greece*, pp. 19ff.; see also Donlan, *The Aristocratic Ideal in Ancient Greece*. In his essay, "The Tradition of

Anti-Aristocratic Thought in Early Greek Poetry," *Historia*, 22 (1977), pp. 145–54 and in P. A. L. Greenhalgh, "Aristocracy and Its Advocates in Archaic Greece," *Greece and Rome*, 19 (1972), pp. 190–207, the two sides of the mirror are presented. P. Spahn, *Mittelschicht und Polisbildung* (Frankfurt, 1977), pp. 59–83, discusses the *Adelstaat,* a subject poorly treated in M. T. W. Arnheim, *Aristocracy in Greek Society* (New York, 1977).

25. As J. Gerlach, *Aner Agathos* (Diss. Munich, 1932), showed that term did not yet have a class significance in the seventh century; in Hesiod and even in Archilochus bravery and beauty do not necessarily go hand in hand.

26. Plutarch, *On Noble Birth* 2 (G. N. Bernardakis, *Moralia*, 8 [Leipzig, 1896]), *Odyssey* 4. 62–64; Archilochus fr. 195 (cf. fr. 65).

27. Sappho fr. 155. A. E. Raubitschek, *Dedications from the Athenian Acropolis* (Cambridge, Mass., 1949), pp. 464–67, is thoughtful on the difficulty in distinguishing aristocrats in epigraphic evidence due to the lack of titles.

28. Three fairly recent essays on aristocratic education bear more on the classic period (and are unfavorable to elites): R. R. Bolgar in R. Wilkinson, ed., *Governing Elites* (New York, 1969), pp. 23–49; R. Seager in F. C. Jaher, ed., *The Rich, The Well Born and the Powerful* (Urbana, Ill., 1975), pp. 7–26; E. C. Welskopf, "Elitevorstellungen und Elitebildung in der hellenischen Polis," *Klio*, 43–45 (1965), pp. 49–64. H. I. Marrou, *History of Education in Antiquity* (New York, 1956), pp. 5–13, 43–44, is more objective.

29. D. L. Page, *Sappho and Alcaeus* (Oxford, 1955), pp. 170–71.

30. 1. 5 1095b; 9. 2 1165a; 10. 8 1179a.

31. H. Troyat, *Pushkin* (New York, 1950), p. 13, quoted by R. Redfield, *The Primitive World and Its Transformations* (Ithaca, 1953), p. 40; another modern parallel is G. Bazin, *The Baroque* (Greenwich, Conn., 1968), p. 322.

32. H. W. Pleket, "Zur Soziologie des antiken Sports," *Mededelingen van het Nederlands Instituut te Rome*, 36 (1974), pp. 57–87.

33. *Works and Days* 20 ff.; Archilochus fr. 29; Alcaeus Z 37; Solon fr. 1.

34. A. Aymard, "Mercenariat et histoire grecque," *Annales de l'Est*, 22 (1959), pp. 16–27.

35. *Economic and Social Growth of Early Greece*, pp. 51–53; Salmon, *Wealthy Corinth*, pp. 149–51, also discusses the place of aristocrats in overseas trade and their replacement by more commercially oriented traders.

36. *Athenaion Politeia* 2; on Roman problems, my *Beginnings of Imperial Rome* (Ann Arbor, 1980), p. 46.

37. My essay, "The Decline of the Early Greek Kings," *Historia,* 10 (1961), pp. 128–38 (*Essays on Ancient History,* pp. 134–43), received its Marxist critique in P. Oliva, "Patrike Basileia," *Geras* (Prague, 1963), pp. 171–81; F. Gschnitzer, "Basileus," *Innsbrucker Beiträge zur Kultur-Wissenschaft,* 11 (1965), pp. 99–112.

38. Athenaeus 6. 258f–259f; G. L. Huxley, *The Early Ionians* (London, 1966), p. 48, dates the event *ca.* 700.

39. Aristotle, *Politics* 3. 9. 7 1285b.

40. E. Will, *Korinthiaka* (Paris, 1955), pp. 295ff., who notes that Strabo 8. 378 stresses the profits of the Bacchiads from controlling the *emporium,* but also firmly emphasizes their rural base (pp. 306–19); Salmon, *Wealthy Corinth,* pp. 55–74.

41. Busolt, *Griechische Staatskunde,* 1, pp. 353ff., remains the fullest and most judicious treatment of Greek constitutional machinery in many varied local forms; see also L. Whibley, *Greek Oligarchies* (London, 1896), and more briefly V. Ehrenberg, *The Greek State* (Norton paperback, 1964), pp. 52ff.

42. Athenaeus 10. 425a; R. Martin, *Recherches sur l'agora grecque* (Paris, 1951); as D. W. Roller, *American Journal of Archaeology,* 78 (1974), p. 154, shows *agoras* could be linear as well as rectangular (or nearly so). A von Gerkan's theory, *Griechische Städteanlagen* (Berlin, 1924), that the *agora* reflects democratic principles as against aristocratic acropoleis is adequately disproven by A. Wokalek, *Griechische Stadtbefestigungen* (Bonn, 1973), pp. 13ff.

43. Gschnitzer, *Griechische Sozialgeschichte,* p. 71; Archilochus fr. 15; Forrest, *Cambridge Ancient History,* 3. 3, pp. 255–56.

44. L. A. Schneider, "Zur sozial Bedeutung der Korai-Statuen," *Hamburger Beiträge zur Archäologie,* Beiheft 2 (1972), unfortunately promises more than is given. In *Thronende und Sitzender Götter* (Bonn, 1982), pp. 133–38, H. Jung comments on the increase in epic themes and figures in art at the beginning of the sixth century (and also in the poetry of Stesichorus, one may note) as an alternative to the aristocratic ideal proper as the sole scale of values. The relation between arts and letters and aristocracy deserves more careful thought.

45. *Paideia,* 1, p. 25.

46. *Politics* 2. 7. 7 1272b.

Chapter V

1. Braun, *Cambridge Ancient History,* 3. 3, pp. 38–39, and Cook, pp. 215–17, emphasize this growth; Snodgrass has reserves on trade narrowly defined as "the purchase and movement of goods without the knowledge or identification of a further purchaser" in *Trade in the Ancient Economy,* edd. P. Garnsey, K. Hopkins, and C. R. Whittaker (London, 1983), pp. 21–26.

2. J. Schumpeter, *Capitalism, Socialism and Democracy* (3d ed.; London, 1950), p. 145.

3. G 2; Page, *Sappho and Alcaeus,* pp. 169ff., and Podlecki, *Early Greek Poets,* pp. 62–88.

4. Cleomenes exiled 700 Athenian families (Herodotus 5. 72); E. Balogh, *Political Refugees in Ancient Greece from the Period of the Tyrants to Alexander the Great* (Johannesburg, 1941), is not very useful.

5. Plutarch, *Greek Questions* 18 and 59 (*Moralia* 295 c–d, 304 e–f); Legon, *Megara,* pp. 119–20.

6. Herodotus 5. 28–29; Plutarch, *Greek Questions* 32 (*Moralia* 298c); Athenaeus 12. 524a; Cook, *Cambridge Ancient History,* 2. 2, p. 800.

7. Meiggs and Lewis, *Greek Historical Inscriptions,* no. 8, with a discussion of recent interpretations.

8. T. J. Dunbabin, *The Western Greeks* (Oxford, 1948), pp. 312–13 on Acragas; H. Drerup, *Griechische Baukunst in geometrischer Zeit* (*Archaeologica Homerica* 2. 0, 1969), pp. 97–99.

9. R. E. Wycherley, *How the Greeks Built Cities* (2d ed.; Norton paperback, 1976); A. Giuliano, *Urbanistica delle città greche* (Milan, 1966); R. Martin, *L'Urbanisme dans la Grèce antique* (Paris, 1956); G. Nenci, "Spazio civico, spazio religioso, spazio catastale nella Polis," *Annali della Scuola Normale Superiore di Pisa,* 9 (1979), pp. 449–477; cf. the ceremonial functions of Chinese centers, stressed by P. Wheatley, *The Pivot of the Four Quarters* (Edinburgh, 1971), who also notes the lack of sharp distinction between the city and its *territorium* (on which also, *La Città e il suo territorio,* Atti del settimo convegno di studi sulla Magna Grecia, 1967; Naples 1968).

10. Busolt, *Griechische Staatskunde,* 1, p. 163, citing Aristotle, fr. 517 V. Rose (Leipzig, 1886); at Athens, A. W. Gomme, *The Population of Athens in the Fifth and Fourth Centuries B.C.* (Oxford, 1933), pp. 37–39. As J. Boardman, *Athenian Red Figure Vases: The Archaic Period* (London, 1975), p. 221, observes, red-figure painters emphasize the city far more than did their black-figure predecessors.

11. C. W. Roebuck, "Some Aspects of Urbanization in Corinth," *Hesperia,* 41 (1972), pp. 96–127; but Salmon, *Wealthy Corinth,* pp. 79–80, would date the appearance of a true city as early as the mid-seventh century.

12. *Economic and Social Growth of Early Greece,* pp. 104–05; F. Frost, *American Journal of Ancient History,* 1 (1976), p. 67; Wokalek, *Griechische Stadtbefestigungen;* F. E. Winter, *Greek Fortifications* (Toronto, 1971). Whether Athens had a city wall before the Persian war is very doubtful despite Herodotus 9. 13, Thucydides 1. 80; cf. E. Vanderpool, *Phoros* (Locust Valley, N.Y., 1976), pp. 156–60.

13. *Economic and Social Growth of Early Greece,* p. 107; M. I. Finley, "The Ancient City," *Comparative Studies in Society and History,* 19 (1977), pp. 305–27; K. Hopkins, "Economic Growth and Towns in Classical Antiquity," *Towns in Societies,* edd. P. Abrams and E. A. Wrigley (Cambridge, 1978), pp. 35–77. In "The Classical City," a paper to be published in his forthcoming *Roman Corinth,* D. W. Engels argues that we should conceive ancient cities as service centers rather than consumer cities. The "core" theory sketched by D. R. Vining Jr., *Scientific American,* December 1982, pp. 44–53, as leading to economic and demographic concentration when a society develops may be relevant here; even more useful is central place theory as discussed by B. J. L. Berry, *The Geography of Market Centers and Retail Distribution* (Englewood Cliffs, N.J., 1967).

14. Cook, *Cambridge Ancient History,* 3. 3, p. 216; F. Braudel, *Capitalism and Material Life 1400–1800* (New York, 1973), pp. 20–21, 375–77, notes that in fifteenth-century Germany an urban center of 3000 required the agricultural surplus of 8.5 square kilometers; in view of lower yields in the Greek landscape this must have then been a minimum.

15. Munich, Antikensammlungen 2307 (A. Furtwängler and R. Reichhold, *Griechische Vasenmalerei* [Munich, 1904], p. 14); M. M. Eisman, "Attic Kyathos Production," *Archaeology,* 28 (1975), pp. 76–83, and in other studies shows that Nicosthenes produced vases intentionally for the Etruscan market.

16. G. K. Jenkins, *Ancient Greek Coins* (London, 1972), p. 9; Herodotus 1. 94. D. Kagan, "The Dates of the Earliest Coins," *American Journal of Archaeology,* 86 (1982), pp. 343–60, seeks to adjust upward the dates of the first coins but is adequately rebutted by J. H. Kroll and N. M. Waggoner, "Dating the Earliest Coins of Athens, Corinth and Aegina," in the same journal, 88 (1984), pp. 325–40.

17. C. M. Kraay, *Archaic and Classical Greek Coins* (Berkeley, 1976),

pp. 317–22, sums up his decisive article, "Hoards, Small Change and the Origin of Coinage," *Journal of Hellenic Studies,* 84 (1964), pp. 76–91.

18. A. Boeckh, *Die Staatshaushaltung der Athener,* 1 (3d ed.; Munich, 1886), p. 181; yet land taxes could exist (Busolt, *Griechische Staatskunde,* 1, p. 610). The concept of coinage as an aid in accounting is advanced by Murray, *Early Greece,* p. 225.

19. J. D. Gould, *Growth in Economic History* (London, 1972), pp. 218–19; *Inscriptiones Graecae* 13. 9, 1273; Meiggs and Lewis, *Greek Historical Inscriptions,* no. 8 (= Jeffery, *Annual of the British School at Athens,* 51 [1956], pp. 157–67). The 2000 staters given by Lydia to Alcaeus and his fellow plotters (fr. 69) were certainly bullion.

20. Raubitschek, *Dedications from the Athenian Acropolis,* no. 178.

21. A. Capizzi, *La repubblica cosmica* (Rome, 1982), pp. 126–29.

22. Archytas B 3 (H. Diels and W. Kranz, *Die Fragmente der Vorsokrater,* 1 [6th ed.; Berlin, 1951], p. 437); Solon fr. 10.

23. L. Mumford, *The Culture of Cities* (New York, 1938), p. 5; Simonides fr. 95.

24. H. W. Parke and D. E. W. Wormell, *The Delphic Oracle,* 1 (Oxford, 1956), pp. 82–83; T. Kelly, *A History of Argos to 500 B.C.* (Minneapolis, 1976), p. 129, would prefer an early sixth-century date.

25. Murray, *Early Greece,* p. 168; as he notes on p. 159 Sparta became unique in that all full citizens were thenceforth hoplites.

26. P. A. Rahe, "The Selection of Ephors at Sparta," *Historia* 29 (1980), pp. 385–401; Ehrenberg, *From Solon to Socrates,* pp. 40ff., emphasizes the role of the ephors.

27. In "The Traditional Enmity between Sparta and Argos," *American Historical Review,* 75 (1970), pp. 971–1003, and "Did the Argives Defeat the Spartans at Hysiae in 669 B.C.?" *American Journal of Philology,* 91 (1970), pp. 31–42, T. Kelly shows conclusively that Spartan-Argive hostility arose only in the sixth century.

28. M. I. Finley, "Sparta," *Problèmes de la guerre en Grèce ancienne,* ed. J. P. Vernant (Paris, 1968), pp. 143–60, who also dates the reorganization to the sixth century.

29. Salmon, *Wealthy Corinth,* pp. 102, 109–10, sums up the evidence for the decline of overseas sale of Corinthian pottery beginning *ca.* 575 and very evident by 550.

30. R. Joffroy, *Le Trésor de Vix* (Paris, 1954); R. M. Cook, *Journal of Hellenic Studies,* 99 (1979), pp. 154–55; J. Boardman, *The Greeks Overseas* (rev. ed.; London, 1980), p. 221. See the trenchant objec-

tions to the conventional view by R. M. Cook, "Spartan History and Archaeology," *Classical Quarterly*, 12 (1962), pp. 156–58; P. Janni, *La cultura di Sparta arcaica* (Rome 1968).

31. Spahn, *Mittelschicht*, p. 110. Thucydides 4. 80, recounting the murder of 2000 helots, is a propaganda story of warfare; if it were true, how could Brasidas have been sent to northern Greece with only helots, equipped moreover as *hoplites?* The distinction between Messenian and Spartan helots is discussed by J. Chambers, *The Historian*, 40 (1978), pp. 271–85.

32. *A Study of History*, 3 (London, 1934), p. 88; G. E. M. de Ste Croix, *The Origins of the Peloponnesian War* (Ithaca, 1972), gives an equally biased picture.

33. Murray, *Early Greece*, p. 177; L. H. Jeffery, *Archaic Greece* (London, 1976), p. 84; Snodgrass, *Archaic Greece*, p. 23, finds "a slight net emigration from the town to the country." Andrewes, always judicious, does not mention the hypothesis in his treatment of early Athens, *Cambridge Ancient History*, 3. 3. There are two somewhat puzzling lines of activity of Athens abroad in the time of Solon: 1) an attack on Sigeum (Page, *Sappho and Alcaeus*, pp. 152–61, based on Herodotus 5. 94 and other evidence which supports a date about 607/6); 2) Athenian intervention in the First Sacred War about 591, as a result of which Athens received a seat on the Delphic amphictyony—but N. Robertson, "The Myth of the First Sacred War," *Classical Quarterly*, n. s. (1978), pp. 38–73, has sought to show that this war was a later invention.

34. Ruschenbusch, *Solonos Nomoi* F 76a, allowing demes, phratries, orgeones if not banned by *demosia grammata*. R. Stroud, *Drakon's Law on Homicide* (Berkeley, 1968); D. M. MacDonald, *Athenian Homicide Law in the Age of the Orators* (Manchester, 1963).

35. Andrewes, *Cambridge Ancient History* 3. 3, pp. 375ff., is the latest treatment. W. Jaeger's essay on Solon's concept of *eunomia* is now available in *Five Essays* (Montreal, 1966).

36. Fr. 1, lines 63ff. A "law of Solon" which purportedly limited the size of farms (Ruschenbusch F 66) is generally rejected.

37. Ruschenbusch F 56.

38. Ruschenbusch F 38; Lysias 31. 127–28. J. A. Goldstein, "Solon's Law for an Activist Citizenry," *Historia*, 21 (1972), pp. 538–45, and B. Manville, "Solon's Law of Stasis and *Atimia* in Archaic Athens," *Transactions of the American Philological Association*, 110 (1980), pp. 213–21, seek to get around the difficulty.

39. J. H. Kroll, "From Wappenmünzen to Owls," *American Numismatic*

Society Museum Notes, 26 (1981), pp. 1–32, building on C. M. Kraay, "The Archaic Owls of Athens," Numismatic Chronicle, 6. ser. 16 (1956), pp. 43–68. Still obdurate is H. A. Cahn, Kleine Schriften zur Münzkunde und Archäologie (Basel, 1975), pp. 81–97.

40. Murray, Early Greece, p. 191 (his whole discussion of Solon, pp. 173–91, is one to which I am indebted).

41. H. Berve, Die Tyrannis bei den Griechen, 2 vols. (Munich, 1967), is the fullest treatment; K. H. Kinzl, Die ältere Tyrannis bis zu den Perserkriegen (Darmstadt, 1979), is a useful collection of recent essays.

42. P. N. Ure, The Origin of Tyranny (Cambridge, 1922); A. Andrewes, The Greek Tyrants (London, 1956), p. 34.

43. P. Oliva, "Die Bedeutung der frühgriechischen Tyrannis," Die ältere Tyrannis, pp. 236–44; E. Kluwe, pp. 281–97; H. W. Pleket, "The Archaic Tyrannis," Talanta, 1 (1969), pp. 19–61; Berve, p. 9, speaks of personal ambition but on p. 10 of the distress of the lower classes.

44. E. Luttwak, Coup d'état (Harvard paperback, 1979), p. 37.

45. Ruschenbusch, Untersuchungen, p. 18, properly stresses this fact.

46. The dates of the Cypselids are those of Salmon, Wealthy Corinth, p. 186; S. Oost, "Cypselus the Bacchiad," Classical Philology, 67 (1972), pp. 10–30; but I remain doubtful. Will, Korinthiaka, pp. 363ff., argued for 610–540; so too K. J. Beloch, Griechische Geschichte, 1 (Strassburg, 1913), pp. 274–82.

47. Kinzl, Die ältere Tyrannis, p. 307, doubts that Orthagoras existed.

48. Herodotus 5.92b2 = Parke and Wormell, Delphic Oracle, no. 7.

49. R. Drews, "The First Tyrants in Greece," Historia, 21 (1972), pp. 129–44, discusses the role of mercenaries and otherwise is among the soundest recent treatments of tyranny.

50. Politics 5. 8. 6 1311a; the means are discussed in 5. 8. 7ff. 1311a. In 5. 8. 2 1310b he states that "tyrants are drawn from the populace and the masses" to protect the demos against the nobles; both the social origins and the aims of actual tyrants can scarcely be reconciled with this view.

51. Ps-Plato, Hipparchus 228C; A. J. Podlecki, "Festivals and Flattery," Athenaeum, 58 (1980), pp. 371–95.

52. E. J. Owens, Journal of Hellenic Studies, 102 (1982), pp. 222–25; U. Jantzen et al., "Die Wasserleitung des Eupalinos," Archäologischer Anzeiger, 88 (1973), pp. 72–89; B. Dunkley, "Greek Fountain-

Buildings before 300 B.C." *Annual of the British School at Athens,* 36 (1935–36), pp. 142–204.

53. Aristotle fr. 611. 20 Rose; Salmon, *Wealthy Corinth,* pp. 133–34, 137, 219–21, 228.

54. J. Boardman, *Revue archéologique* 1972, pp. 57–72, and *Journal of Hellenic Studies,* 95 (1975), pp. 1–12, notes the appearance of the motif of Athena escorting Heracles on vases and argues a Pisistratid connection; in "Exekias," *American Journal of Archaeology,* 82 (1978), pp. 11–25, he suggests that this potter subtly commented on tyranny. Both seem to be very doubtful.

55. Jeffery, *Archaic Greece,* p. 147; Murray, *Early Greece,* pp. 140ff., also overstresses the role of trade, as does A. French, *The Growth of the Athenian Economy* (London, 1964), pp. 33ff., with regard to Pisistratus' interest in the city of Athens.

56. Hignett, *Athenian Constitution,* p. 115, and Sealey, *History of the Greek City States,* p. 139, think some distribution of the lands of exiled nobles probable; Andrewes, *Cambridge Ancient History,* 3. 3., p. 406, is firm that we have no evidence. The clearest suggestion is at Corinth (Herodotus 5. 92e2); and Will, *Korinthiaka,* pp. 477–81, argues for such distribution. Salmon, *Wealthy Corinth,* p. 195, is dubious.

57. Pollux, *Onomasticon,* Z. 68; Salmon, *Wealthy Corinth,* pp. 199–203, is too sceptical about such rules.

58. L. Gernet, "Mariages de tyrans," *Anthropologie de la Grèce antique* (Paris, 1968), pp. 344–59.

59. The conventional ancient picture that he strove to reduce the role of Dorians is more than suspect; see E. Will, *Doriens et Ioniens* (Strasbourg, 1956), pp. 39ff., and A. Griffin, *Sikyon* (Oxford, 1982), pp. 37–38, 50.

60. Aristotle, *Politics* 5. 9. 2 1315b.

61. Berve, *Die Tyrannis,* pp. 177ff.

62. W. W. How and J. Wells, *A Commentary on Herodotus,* 2 (Oxford, 1928), p. 339; A. Ferrill, "Herodotus on Tyranny," *Historia,* 27 (1978), pp. 385–98.

63. Nicolaus of Damascus, *Die Fragmente der griechischen Historiker,* ed. F. Jacoby, 2. A (Berlin, 1926), 90 F 60. 1, as translated by Salmon, *Wealthy Corinth,* p. 229; M. Ostwald, "The Athenian Legislation against Tyranny and Subversion," *Transactions of the American Philological Association,* 86 (1955), pp. 103–28.

64. The official decree on the founding of Brea made its leader autocrat:

Meiggs and Lewis, *Greek Historical Inscriptions,* no. 49, lines 8–9.
65. Fr. 33 (context unknown and not necessarily political).
66. Busolt, *Griechische Staatskunde,* 1, p. 601; Andreades, *Greek Public Finance,* 1, p. 121.

Chapter VI

1. I owe the happy term "check-list" to Pounds, *Annals of the Association of American Geographers,* 59 (1969), p. 139; Pausanias 10. 4. 1 gives a specific example.
2. So Aristotle, *Politics* 3. 6. 13 1282b; shortly thereafter he defines law as "reason free from all passion."
3. F. Gschnitzer, *Abhängige Örte im griechischen Altertum* (Munich, 1958); M. Amit, *Great and Small Poleis* (Brussels, 1973).
4. The fundamental articles are by J. A. O. Larsen, "Sparta and the Ionian Revolt," *Classical Philology,* 27 (1932), pp. 136–50, and "The Constitution of the Peloponnesian League," *Classical Philology,* 28 (1933), pp. 257–76; 29 (1934), pp. 1–10; Ste Croix, *Origins of the Peloponnesian War,* pp. 101–24, is a careful analysis. See also L. Moretti, *Richerche sulle leghe greche* (Rome, 1962); part of one treaty has recently been discovered, F. Gschnitzer, *Ein neuer spartanischer Staatsvertrag und die Verfassung des Peloponnesisches Bundes* (Meissenheim, 1978).
5. J. K. Davies, *Athenian Propertied Families 600–300 B. C.* (Oxford, 1971), p. 374.
6. Herodotus 3. 137.
7. *Athenaion Politeia* 13. 5 suggests that this revision of the citizen rolls was accepted by Cleisthenes; so Pleket, *Talanta,* 4 (1972), p. 73, and D. W. Knight, *Historia* Einzelschrift 13 (1970), pp. 15–24; see also J. H. Oliver, *Historia* 9 (1960), pp. 503–97, vs. D. Kagan, *Historia,* 12 (1963), pp. 41–46.
8. Herodotus 5. 66; *Athenaion Politeia* 20; M. Ostwald, *Autonomia* (American Philological Association, 1982).
9. Herodotus and *Athenaion Politeia* are in conflict here; Herodotus suggests that the council of 500 had been established by the time of Cleomenes' intervention. Modern scholars also disagree: Hignett, *Athenian Constitution,* pp. 126–27; Ostwald, *Nomos,* p. 143; Pleket, *Talanta,* 4 (1972), pp. 74–76; Meier, *Die Entstehung des Politischen,* pp. 91–143, has an extended discussion of the reforms.
10. J. S. Traill, *The Political Organization of Attica, Hesperia* Supplement 14 (1975); C. W. J. Eliot, *Coastal Demes of Attika, Phoenix*

Supplement 5 (1962); P. Siewert, *Die Trittyen Attikas und die Heeresreform des Kleisthenes, Vestigia,* 33 (1982); new evidence on the boundaries of some trittyes is given by Traill, *Hesperia* Supplement 19 (1982), pp. 162–71.

11. Meiggs and Lewis, *Greek Historical Inscriptions,* no. 85.

12. P. J. Rhodes, *The Athenian Boule* (Oxford, 1972); R. de Laix, *Probouleusis at Athens* (Berkeley, 1973); E. S. Staveley, *Greek and Roman Voting and Elections* (Ithaca, 1972), pp. 52–54.

13. J. D. Lewis, "Isegoria at Athens: When Did It Begin?" *Historia,* 20 (1971), pp. 129–40; G. T. Griffith, *Ancient Society and Institutions,* pp. 115–38.

14. This geographical awareness is emphasized by P. Lévêque and P. Vidal-Naquet, *Clisthène l'Athénien* (Paris, 1964); I have considered the more precise consciousness of space in *The Awakening of the Greek Historical Spirit* (New York, 1968), pp. 41–49.

15. Salmon, *Wealthy Corinth,* pp. 207–09, 413–19; N. F. Jones, "The Civic Organization of Corinth," *Transactions of the American Philological Association,* 110 (1980), pp. 161–93; on east Greece see Cook, *Cambridge Ancient History,* 3. 3., pp. 200–01.

16. Spahn, *Mittelschicht,* pp. 163–67; Ostwald, *Nomos,* p. 153; B. Haussoullier, *La vie municipale en Attique* (Paris, 1884).

17. So D. M. Lewis, "Cleisthenes and Attica," *Historia,* 12 (1963), pp. 22–40; D. W. Bradeen, "The Trittyes in Cleisthenes' Reforms," *Transactions of the American Philological Association,* 86 (1955), pp. 22–30; R. J. Hopper, " 'Plain,' 'Shore,' and 'Hill' in Early Athens," *Annual of the British School at Athens,* 56 (1961), pp. 189–219. Family politics are still visible in the fifth century: G. Daverio Rocchi, "Politica di familia e politica di tribù nella polis ateniese (V secolo)," *Acme,* 24 (1972), pp. 13–44.

18. J. R. Ellis and G. R. Stanton, "Factional Conflict and Solon's Reforms," *Phoenix,* 22 (1968), pp. 95–110.

19. R. Seager's summation of Meier, *Die Entstehung des Politischen,* in *Journal of Hellenic Studies,* 102 (1982), pp. 266–67; see also H. W. Pleket, "Isonomia and Cleisthenes, A Note," *Talanta,* 4 (1972), pp. 64–81; J. Martin, *Chiron,* 4 (1974), pp. 5–42.

20. E. R. Wolf, *Peasants* (Englewood Cliffs, N.J., 1966), p. 11.

21. Well discussed in G. Mingay, *The Gentry* (London, 1976); E. Wingfield-Stratton, *The Squire and His Relations* (London, 1956).

22. S. I. Oost, "The Megara of Theagenes and Theognis," *Classical Philology,* 68 (1973), pp. 186–96; G. Cerri, "La terminologia sociopolitica di Theognide," *Quaderni Urbinati,* 6 (1968), pp. 7–32; more

generally, M. L. West, *Studies in Greek Elegy and Iambus* (Berlin, 1974), chaps. 3 and 4.

23. Theognis 847–50; Donlan, *Parola del Passato,* 25 (1970), p. 393.

24. Donlan, *Aristocratic Ideal,* p. 77.

25. M. Detienne has analyzed the meaning of *to meson* in Herodotus, tragedy, and elsewhere in "En Grèce archaïque: géométrie, politique et société," *Annales,* 20 (1965), pp. 425–41; and *Les Maîtres de vérité dans la Grèce archaïque* (Paris, 1967), pp. 88–99; see also Ostwald, *Nomos,* pp. 107–08, and Rahe, *American Historical Review,* 89 (1984), p. 282.

26. *Odyssey,* 7. 310; Hesiod, *Works and Days* 694. Oddly enough Spahn, *Mittelschicht,* pays little attention to this concept and cites Phocylides, for example, only casually on p. 153.

27. Phocylides fr. 12; Theognis 219–20, 331–32, 335–36, 945–48.

28. *Suppliants* 238ff.; Pindar, *Pythian* 11. 50–53.

29. So Finley, *Politics,* p. 10, dismisses the concept of a fictitious middle class on which Meier and Spahn in his judgment have erroneously built; but this disregards the evidence for a political *stance* of "the middle"; see Greenhalgh, *Greece and Rome,* 19 (1972), pp. 199–200. Aristotle, *Politics* 4. 4. 9 1295b is to be understood in this sense.

30. *Politics* 4. 3 1289b; in 4. 4 1293a limits on assembly; in 5.7 1308b–1309a a state is called democratic in structure but oligarchic in practice.

31. Ruschenbusch, *Untersuchungen,* pp. 24ff.

32. J. A. O. Larsen, "The Origin and Significance of the Counting of Votes," *Classical Philology,* 44 (1949), pp. 164–81, finds the origins as early as Solon; on actual voting procedures in later Athens, A. Boegehold, *Hesperia,* 32 (1963), pp. 366–74.

33. P. A. Rahe, "The Primacy of Politics in Classical Greece," *American Historical Review,* 89 (1984), pp. 265–93, discusses the different position of citizens in Greek states and in modern political theory. As Meier, *Die Entstehung des Politischen,* p. 45, put it, the political side of life eventually became the "zentrales Lebenselement"; the rise of this consciousness is the central theme of his study.

34. K. Minogue, *Encounter* June 1984, p. 31.

35. *Force and Freedom* (New York, 1943), ch. VI = *Philosophy of History in Our Time,* ed. H. Meyerhoff (Doubleday paperback, 1959), p. 280.

Bibliography

Sources

For the texts of the epics I have relied on the Oxford editions; for Hesiod, the new edition by M. L. West (Oxford, 1978), and for translation that of H. G. Evelyn-White (Loeb Classical Library). Fragments of the early poets are given in the numeration of E. Diehl's edition (3 vols.; 3d ed., Leipzig, 1952–55) save for Archilochus, cited from F. Lasserre and A. Bonnard (Paris, 1958), and for Sappho and Alcaeus, E. Lobel and D. Page (Oxford, 1955). Translations of Herodotus and Thucydides are usually from the Penguin vouumes of A. de Selincourt and Rex Warner; texts are those of the Oxford editions. Aristotle's works are cited by the running heads in the Teubner texts; the translation of the *Politics* is that of E. Barker. Inscriptions are given from the most recent publications; as far as possible that of R. Meiggs and D. Lewis (Oxford, 1969).

Modern Works

The following bibliography is rigorously selective and lists, above all, the most recent works. Treatments of specific topics such as tyranny, coinage, or public buildings are covered by notes in the text; full references to economic and social developments can be found in my *Economic and Social Growth of Early Greece, 800–500 B.C.* (New York, 1977).

Political Structure

Boeckh, A., *Die Staatshaushaltung der Athener,* 2 vols. (3d ed.; Munich, 1886).

Busolt, G., *Griechische Staatskunde,* 2 vols. (3d ed.; Munich, 1920–26).
Ehrenberg, V., *The Greek State* (Norton paperback, 1964).
Fustel de Coulanges, *La Cité antique* (Paris, 1864).
Hignett, C., *A History of the Athenian Constitution to the End of the Fifth Century B.C.* (Oxford, 1952).

Political History and Practice

Beloch, G., *Griechische Geschichte,* 3 vols. (2d ed.; Strassburg/Berlin, 1912–23).
Boardman, J., *The Greeks Overseas* (rev. ed.; London, 1980).
Cambridge Ancient History, 2. 2 (Cambridge, 1975); 3. 1 (1982), 3. 3 (1982).
Coldstream, J. N., *Geometric Greece* (New York, 1977).
Ehrenberg, V., *From Solon to Socrates* (London, 1968).
Finley, M. I., *Early Greece: The Bronze and Archaic Ages* (New York, 1970).
———, *Politics in the Ancient World* (Cambridge paperback, 1983).
———, *The World of Odysseus* (rev. ed.; New York, 1978).
Jeffery, L. H., *Archaic Greece* (London, 1976).
Lintott, A., *Violence, Civil Strife and Revolution in the Classical City 750–330 B.C.* (London, 1982).
Meier, C., *Die Entstehung des Politischen bei den Griechen* (Frankfurt, 1980).
Murray, O., *Early Greece* (Atlantic Highlands, N.J., 1980).
Ostwald, M., *Nomos and the Beginnings of the Athenian Democracy* (Oxford, 1969).
Ruschenbusch, E., *Untersuchungen zu Staat und Politik in Griechenland vom 7.-4. Jh. v. Chr.* (Bamberg, 1978).
Sealey, R., *A History of the Greek City States, ca. 700–338 B.C.* (Berkeley, 1976).
Snodgrass, A. M., *The Dark Age of Greece* (Chicago, 1972).
———, *Archaic Greece* (London, 1980).
Spahn, P., *Mittelschicht und Polisbildung* (Frankfurt, 1977).

Specific Poleis and Areas (note that there is no monograph devoted to Athens across our period; it simply swallows up most general histories of Greece, as Ehrenberg, *From Solon to Socrates,* p. 1, stresses at the outset of that work).

Buck, R. J., *A History of Boeotia* (Edmonton, 1979).
Craik, E., *The Dorian Aegean* (London, 1980).

Drögemüller, H. P., *Syrakus* (*Gymnasium* Beiheft 6, 1969).

Dunbabin, T. J., *The Western Greeks* (Oxford, 1948).

Emlyn-Jones, C. J., *The Ionians and Hellenism* (London, 1980).

Forrest, W. G., *A History of Sparta 950–192 B.C.* (Norton paperback, 1969).

Freeman, K., *Greek City-States* (Norton paperback, 1963).

Griffin, A., *Sikyon* (Oxford, 1982).

Huxley, G. L., *The Early Ionians* (London, 1966).

Kelly, T., *A History of Argos to 500 B.C.* (Minneapolis, 1976).

Legon, R. P., *Megara* (Ithaca, 1981).

Renfrew, C., and Wagstaff, M., edd., *An Island Polity: The Archaeology of Exploitation in Melos* (Cambridge, 1982).

Salmon, J. B., *Wealthy Corinth* (Oxford, 1984).

Will, E., *Korinthiaka* (Paris, 1955).

Willetts, R. F., *Aristocratic Society in Ancient Crete* (London, 1955).

Cultural Development

Adkins, A. W. H., *Moral Values and Political Behaviour in Ancient Greece* (New York, 1974).

Bonnard, A., *Greek Civilization* (London, 1957).

Dodds, E. R., *The Greeks and the Irrational* (Beacon paperback, 1957).

Donlan, W., *The Aristocratic Ideal in Archaic Greece* (Lawrence, Kans., 1980).

Fränkel, H., *Early Greek Poetry and Philosophy* (Oxford, 1975).

Gschnitzer, F., *Griechische Sozialgeschichte von der mykenischen bis zum Ausgang der klassischen Zeit* (Wiesbaden, 1981).

Hägg, R., ed., *The Greek Renaissance of the Eighth Century B.C.* (Stockholm, 1983).

Lesky, A., *A History of Greek Literature* (London, 1966).

Jaeger, W., *Paideia,* 3 vols. (Berlin, 1936–55).

Podlecki, A. J., *The Early Greek Poets and Their Times* (Vancouver, 1984).

Starr, C. G., *Awakening of the Greek Historical Spirit* (New York, 1968).

——, *The Origins of Greek Civilization* (New York, 1961).

Anthropological Studies

Fried, M. H., *The Evolution of Political Society* (New York, 1967).

Gluckman, M., *Politics, Law and Ritual in Tribal Society* (Oxford, 1968).

Haas, J., *The Evolution of the Prehistoric State* (New York, 1982).

Humphreys, S., *Anthropology and the Greeks* (London, 1978).

Sahlins, M., *Stone Age Economics* (London, 1972).

————, *Tribesmen* (Englewood Cliffs, N.J., 1968).

Schapera, I., *Tribal Legislation among the Tswana of the Bechuanaland Protectorate* (London, 1943).

Service, E. R., *Origins of the State and Civilization* (Philadelphia, 1978).

Wolf, E. R., *Peasants* (Englewood Cliffs, N.J., 1966).

Index

Accounting, **72**
Acropolis, 3, 56, 73, 90, 97
Administration, public, 59, 65, 85, 87
Aegina, 47, 72
Agora, 19, 25, 31, 40, 60, 65, 70, 83, 90
Agriculture, 5–8, 36, 38–39, 71, 83, 87
Alcaeus, 53, 58, 62–63, 68, 95
Alcman, 49, 53
Alphabet, 57–58
Amphictyony. *See* Leagues
Archilochus, 50, 53–55, 61–63, 65
Archons, 65
Arete, 30, 55, 95
Argos, 10, 47, 49, 64, 74–75, 82
Aristocracy: origins, 30–32, 41; way
    of life, 59–63, 95; political role, 64–
    68, 74, 77–79, 86, 89
Aristotle, 46, 54, 61, 66, 80, 82, 97
Artisans. *See* Industries
Assembly, 18–20, 24–26, 56, 78, 87,
    91–92, 97
Athens (and Attica): general, 3–6, 28,
    37, 40, 54, 67, 87, 97; early history,
    10, 12, 38, 47–49, 56, 60–62, 64, 70–
    71; under Solon, 56, 77–80; under
    Pisistratus, 81–85; democracy, 88–
    93, 98–99

Basileus (pl. *basileis*), 11, 17–26, 35,
    56, 59, 64–65
Boeotia, 3, 13, 48–49, 87, 92

Booty, 23, 30
Boule. See Council
Bouleuterion, 65

Callinus, 53–54
Chalcis, 39, 81, 92
Charondas, 57
Chieftains, 16–18, 43
Chios, 47, 64, 69, 71
Cities, 23, 70–72
Citizens, 79, 89, 91, 93, 98–100
Clan. *See Genos*
Class conflict, 43–45, 66–69, 77–78, 97
Cleomenes, 88, 90
Cleisthenes (of Athens), 88–93
Cleisthenes (of Sicyon), 81, 83–84
Climate, 5–6
Coinage, 47, 56, 72–73, 79–80, 83, 87
Colonization (and colonies), 10, 34,
    36, 38, 41, 57, 67, 70, 85
Corinth: general, 4, 10, 39, 47, 49, 56,
    65, 91; clay products, 5, 34, 58,
    76; economic role, 70, 72–73, 83;
    under Cypselids, 81–82, 84–85
Crete, 11–12, 57, 66, 94
Council, 20, 25, 56, 65, 69, 78, 87,
    91–92
Cylon, 56, 81
Cyprus, 12, 64
Cypselus (and Cypselids), 81–84, 88

Dark Ages, 15–16, 22–23, 30–32
Delos, 40, 59, 84
Delphi, 50, 55, 59, 69, 74, 82, 84, 90
Demes, 90, 92
Demos, 23, 26, 44, 56–57, 69, 79, 81,
    95
Dike. *See* Justice
Draco, 57, 78

Ecclesia. *See* Assembly
Egypt, 12, 63, 88
Eisphora. *See* Taxes
Eleusis, 47–48, 84
Ephesus, 4
Ephors, 75
Eretria, 39–40, 81
Ethnos. *See* Tribes as political units
Eunomia, 55, 79

Family, 4, 8. *See also* *Kleros; Oikos*
Farms, size of, 7, 13
Festivals, 40
Foundries. *See* Metals (and metal-
    working)

Generals, 54–55, 65
Genos, 29
Gift exchange, 31–32
Grain trade, 6, 71
Guest friendship, 61
Gulf of Corinth, 5, 10, 73, 82

Harbor works, 73, 83
Helots, 76
Herodotus, 39, 48, 56, 72, 85, 92, 97
Hesiod, 6, 9, 17, 25, 30, 34, 50, 63, 93
Homer, 16–17, 84
Hoplite class, 54, 80–81

Industries, 71, 73, 77, 87, 93
Ionia, 35

Ischia, 36
Isonomia, 90
Italy, 12, 34, 41, 88

Justice, 22, 24–25, 73, 96

Kakoi, 26, 60, 63, 94–95
King. *See Basileus*
Kinship, 29–30
Kleros, 8, 26, 28

Laos. *See Demos*
Law courts, 78, 96
Laws, 57–58, 74, 78–79, 85
Leagues, 50, 87–88
Lefkandi, 15
Lydia, 50, 63, 68, 72, 88

Magistrates, 50, 87, 91
Manufacture. *See* Industries
Megara, 39, 47, 49, 68–69, 77, 81–82,
    99
Melos, 9, 38
Mercenaries, 63, 82, 88
Merchants. *See* Trade (and traders)
Messenia, 49, 55, 74–75, 94
Metals (and metalworking), 5, 12,
    16, 36, 41–42, 71, 76
Miletus, 47, 67, 69, 81, 91
Mimnermus, 53
Mytilene, 45, 65, 68
Money. *See* Coinage
Mycenaean age, 11–12, 15

Naucratis, 67
Near East, 10–13, 34, 42, 45, 72

Oikos, 27
Oligarchy, 68–69, 93, 97

Olympia, 59, 62, 76, 84, 97
Orchomenus, 49

Patriotism, 27, 54–55, 98
Peasants, 63–64, 77–78, 83, 93–94
Peloponnesus, 5, 10, 12, 48, 73
Periander, 83–84
Persian empire, 18, 72, 77, 88–89
Phalanx, 54, 80
Pheidon, 49
Phocylides, 58, 94
Phoenicia, 42, 93
Phratry, 23, 28, 91
Phyle. See Tribes as political
    division
Piracy, 12, 53
Piraeus, 3, 10
Pisistratus (and sons), 68, 80–85, 88,
    90
Pittacus, 68
Polemarch. See Generals
Polycrates, 81, 83
Population, 8, 15, 38–39, 46–47, 71
Potters (and pottery), 5, 16, 34, 50,
    53, 67, 71, 76, 97
Prytaneion, 7, 48, 65

Religion, 30, 32, 39–40, 49, 58–59, 84

Samos, 39, 47, 62, 69, 76, 81, 83
Sappho, 53, 60, 63, 68, 95
Saronic gulf, 5, 10, 73, 82
Sculpture, 53, 62, 97
Shipping. *See* Trade (and traders)
Sicily, 12, 34, 81, 97
Sicyon, 47, 56, 81, 83, 85, 90–91
Slavery, 12, 26, 71, 93
Solon, 53, 57, 63, 70, 73, 77–80, 93

Sparta: general, 36, 47, 64, 72; early
    history, 47–48; reorganizations, 28,
    55–56, 74–75, 79; under Cleomenes,
    88, 90; place in Greek history, 10,
    76–77
Strategus. See Generals
Symposia, 28, 62, 95
Syracuse, 36, 47, 69
Syria, 12

Taxes, 22, 25, 72, 83
Temples, 34, 39–40, 53, 58, 65, 67
Theagenes, 68, 81, 83
Thebes, 10, 47, 49, 82, 87
Theognis, 94–96
Thessaly, 5, 10, 94
Thucydides, 48, 56, 62
To meson, 96–97
Tolls, harbor, 72, 83
Trade (and traders), 9–10, 42, 63, 67,
    73, 93
Treasuries, 56, 72
Tribes: as political subdivisions, 56,
    84–85, 90–91; as political units, 27,
    35, 37, 50, 87
Tyrants, 57, 60, 76, 80–86, 90
Tyrtaeus, 53, 55, 74

Villages, 3–4, 7–8, 91

War, 22–23, 35, 39, 50, 53–55, 74–77,
    84
Wealth, 13, 22–23, 41, 62–63, 78, 95
Women, 3–4, 8, 28–29, 61, 75, 89

Zaleucus, 57
Zeus, 19, 22, 24–25